OWAIN GLYNDŴR
Prince of Wales

SEPTENTRIO

THE·REALM·OF
PRINCE·OWAIN
GLYNDWR·14·04

Beaumaris
Conway
Rhuddlan
ANGLE-SEY
Bangor
St Asaph
Flint
Chester
Caernarvon
Denbigh
Ruthin
Snowdon
Glyndyfrdwy
Harlech
Berwyn Range
Oswestry
Barmouth
Sycharth
Dolgelley
Shrewsbury
Cader Idris
Machynlleth
Pennel
Severn R.
Mynydd
Hyddgen
Aberystwyth
Plynlimon
Ludlow
Llanbadarn
Pilleth
Strata
Florida
Rhay-
ader
Luge R.
Woodbury
Hill
Cardigan
Teifi R.
Wye R.
Hay
Hereford
Newcastle
Tovy R.
Brecon
Black Mts
Kentchurch
St David's
Llansant-
ffraed
Campston
Carmarthen
Llandeilo
Brecon Beacons
Aberga-
venny
Monmouth
Haverford
Llanstephan
Craigy Dorth
Laugharne
Kidwelly
Abergavenny
Usk
Usk
Tenby
MILFORD
HAVEN
GOWER
Newport
Coity
Cardiff

OCCIDENS

ORIENS

MERIDIES

A SCALE OF MILES
5 10 15 20 25

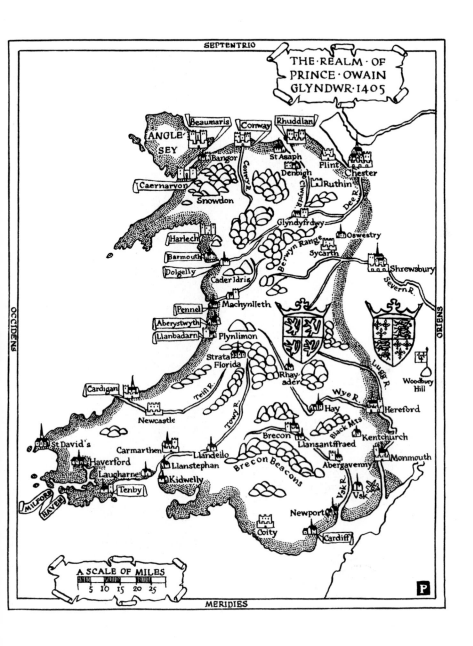

THE·REALM·OF
PRINCE·OWAIN
GLYNDWR·1405

SEPTENTRIO

OCCIDENS

ORIENS

MERIDIES

ANGLE·SEY

Beaumaris
Conway
Rhuddlan
Bangor
St Asaph
Flint
Chester
Denbigh
Caernarvon
Ruthin
Snowdon
Conway R.
Clwyd R.
Dee R.
Glyndyfrdwy
Berwyn Range
Oswestry
Harlech
Sycarth
Barmouth
Shrewsbury
Dolgelly
Severn R.
Cader Idris
Machynlleth
Pennel
Aberystwyth
Llanbadarn
Plynlimon
Strata Florida
Lugg R.
Rhayader
Woodbury Hill
Cardigan
Teifi R.
Wye R.
Hay
Hereford
Newcastle
Towy R.
Brecon
Black Mts
Kentchurch
St David's
Carmarthen
Llandeilo
Llansantffraed
Haverford
Llanstephan
Brecon Beacons
Abergavenny
Monmouth
Laugharne
Kidwelly
Tenby
Usk R.
Usk
MILFORD HAVEN
Newport
Coity
Cardiff

A SCALE OF MILES
5 10 15 20 25

Owain Glyndŵr in full state as Prince of Wales. (By permission of the National Library of Wales.)

OWAIN GLYNDŴR
Prince of Wales

IAN SKIDMORE

CHRISTOPHER DAVIES

FIRST IMPRESSION 1978
SECOND IMPRESSION 1980

PAPERBACK EDITION 1986
REPRINTED 1992, 1996

Published by
Christopher Davies (Publishers) Ltd.
P.O. Box 403
Swansea, SA1 4YF

ISBN 0 7154 0667 1

Printed in Wales by
Dinefwr Press
Rawlings Road, Llandybïe
Dyfed, SA18 3YD

*In memory of my father-in-law, Dr 'Joe' Lucas,
a small return for a precious gift*

LIST OF ILLUSTRATIONS

Frontispiece: *opposite*
   Owain Glyndŵr in full state as Prince of Wales.   *page*

Coronation of Richard II. French school detail 48

The funeral of Richard II, from 'Chroniques
   d'Angleterre', Froissart 49

Old Parliamentary House, Dollgelly (plan) .... page 56

The coronation of Henry Bolinbroke. Detail from an
   illustration in 'Chroniques d'Angleterre', Froissart 64

Archbishop Arundel preaching in the cause of Henry IV... 64

Richard II captured at Flint Castle. A detail from
   Froissart's 'Chronicles' 65

Henry V — artist unknown 100

Harlech Castle, as it might have appeared at the time
   of its completion about 1290 101

Carreg Cennen, as it might have appeared before it
   was dismantled in 1462 116

Siege Warfare 117

Old Parliament House 148

A facsimile of Owen's letter to Charles VI of France,
   stating the position of the Welsh Church as Owen saw it .. 148

Old Parliament House 149

'The Rout of Owain Glyndŵr's army' from 'Life of
   Richard Beauchamp' by John Rous 164

Siôn Kent: from a panel at Kentchurch Court 165

CONTENTS

Chapter   *Page*

I   Barefoot Welsh Doggis   11

II   Owain's Children   31

III   A Matter of Most Evil Precedent   42

IV   Every Man Shall Have Weapons   57

V   An Effusion of Blood   77

VI   The Prince of Priests   94

VII   Better to Die in Battle   121

VIII   Abashed is now the Saxon   137

IX   Fire and the Edge of the Sword   153

X   A Fury of Barbarous Saxons   162

         Appendix A   179

         Appendix B   180

         Bibliography   182

         Index   188

ACKNOWLEDGEMENTS

TO:

My wife Celia who overcame the horrors of translating mediæval Latin and French with characteristic aplomb and revised this manuscript.

Walter Payne, M.A., whose cartographic gifts have enriched many European jaunts and now enhance this book.

Ian Callister without whose help it could never have been written.

Ray Benson, the Chester Reference Librarian and his colleagues whose success in pursuit of obscure works of reference was total.

The Archivists of Chester, Cheshire and Worcester and their patient staffs. The staffs of the Public Record Office and the National Library of Wales.

Colonel John Lucas-Scudamore of Kentchurch Court for permission to use the painting which appears opposite page 165.

Mr Warren Skidmore, the University of Akron, Ohio, U.S.A., for allowing me to make use of his researches into the genealogy of the Scudamore family.

Peter Rowley-Conwy, M.A., for perfectly timed advice and encouragement.

Lynn Hughes, whose sensitive editing belies Dr Johnson's dictum that authors should have as little to do with each other as possible.

THANK YOU

I

BAREFOOT WELSH DOGGIS

T HE KING was dead. His long Plantagenet head, yellow now and marbling, jogged on a black pillow. The litter on which he lay was draped in black and four grooms in black livery led the black horses which drew it through the London streets. Behind the king's body, embalmed in spicery, virgin wax and cummin, encased in lead, perhaps to hide sword wounds, marched four knights in black surcoats. The cart wheels threw up stones from the rough road, marking their black hose with small craters of grey dust.

Behind the knights the London mob swelled and jostled. In the two hours that Richard II's wasted body lay, by the new king's orders, on the cart in Cheapside amid the flies and litter of mediæval London, more than 20,000 of the London commons filed past. It was not a respectful farewell for Richard had not been a popular king. His successor Henry IV was much more to the mob's taste. But it was not every day a man saw a dead king, humbled, and they came in their droves.

There were plump burgesses in the crowd and barons, still uneasy after the recent peasants' revolt, watching the mob warily.

There were bakers and brewers, woollen websters and butchers, masons and tailors. There were soldiers back from the French wars, purses jingling with their indenture pay; ditchers and diggers, whores and thieves, clerks and cooks and sergeants of the King's Bench. They were dressed in a clash of colours and the stench from their bodies rose in a thick cloud. Only the dead king smelled sweet from his spices.

There was a holiday atmosphere. Cooks and their helpers cried 'Pies, Hot Pies', 'Good Pork and Good Goose. Come Dine, Come Dine' and there were queues for the sixpenny stuffed capons, running juice. From the inn doorways, dark and inviting, taverners lured with 'Wine, White from Alsace, Red from Gascony. Wine of the Rhine and Rochelle to help settle your meat.'

Rumour was alive in the patched and dandy crowd. No-one could believe that Richard was dead. Questions about his fate had been asked since Henry, ostensibly bent only on recovering the inheritance of his father John of Gaunt, had captured him, at Flint Castle on the Dee Estuary. It was to answer them once and for all that Henry had ordered this macabre lying in state amid the bustle and noise of Cheapside. Obedient at last, tyrant Richard, the unlikely heir to the Black Prince, returned to his capital with a bodyguard of flies.

To one man, at least, Richard's fall had come as no surprise. Adam of Usk was a Welsh ecclesiastic lawyer with a flourishing London practice. The patronage of Thomas Arundel, the new Archbishop of Canterbury, promised a golden future and he was free to indulge his hobby, the pursuit of heavenly portents.

Adam of Usk saw them everywhere.

When he returned from viewing Richard's corpse he mused on the three ensigns of royalty which had plainly shown him that the Plantagenet would come to a bad end as early as Richard's coronation, more than twenty years earlier.

'First,' Adam recalled in his Chronicle; 'in the procession he lost one of his coronation shoes, whence in the first place the commons who rose up against him hated him ever after his whole life long; secondly one of his golden spurs fell off, whence, in the second place, the soldiers opposed him in rebellion; thirdly, at the banquet a sudden gust of wind carried away the crown from his head, whence, in the third and last place, he was set aside from his kingdom and supplanted by King Henry.'

The prophecies of John of Bridlington were conundrums and burgesses spent hours puzzling such clues as 'When he shall go in with the dog, the lion shall fly with the bull'. To Adam this cryptic clue presented no difficulty. He explained '...The Duke Henry was rightfully the dog, by reason of his badge of a collar of linked greyhounds and because he came in the dog days and because he utterly drove out from the kingdom the faithless harts, that is the livery of King Richard which was the hart.'

He noted the affair of Richard's greyhound which supported his theory.

'I saw with King Henry a greyhound of wonderful nature which, on the death of his master, the Earl of Kent, found its way by its own instinct to King Richard, whom it had never before seen and who was then in distant parts; and withersoever the king went, and wheresoever he stood or lay down, it was ever by his side, with grim and lion-like face, until the same king, as is before told, fled at midnight by stealth and in craven fear from his army; and then, deserting him, and again led by instinct and by itself and with no guide, it came straight from Carmarthen to Shrewsbury to the Duke of Lancaster, now king, who lay at that time in the monastery with his army, and, as I looked on, it crouched before him, whom it had never seen before, with a submissive but bright and pleased aspect. And when the duke heard of its qualities, believing that thereby his good fortune was foretold, he welcomed the hound right willingly, and with joy, and let it sleep upon his bed. And after the setting aside of King Richard, when it was brought to him, it cared not to regard him at all other than as a private man whom it knew not; which the deposed king took sorely to heart.'

†   †   †

If the hound was faithless, Richard's harts remained. Frozen in stone they danced in a string course on the walls of the still unfinished Palace of Westminster where, against a background of masons' scaffolding on a bitterly cold October day, Henry held his first parliament.

Richard's major contribution to civilisation had been the invention of the handkerchief. Before its arrival hands that dipped in shared stews and dainties also blew the nose. Unarguably the handkerchief conferred a greater benefit on civilisation than did the whole of the Hundred Years War, but it was the Palace of Westminster that Richard saw as the apogee of his reign. His architect, Henry Yevele, demolished the wooden Norman stronghold of William Rufus and built on the site a new palace of stone. The hammer-beam roof, the first of its kind and the envy of Europe, had been carved from oaks cut from Richard's estate in Odiham, Hampshire. On the tie beams were the exquisite angels carved by Robert Grassington. The unfinished statues of six kings by Walter Walton flanked the great South Window. But on that October day in 1399 the writ that ran below was Henry's.

The new king was short, with a wide breadth of shoulder. He had heavy hooded eyes and a thick moustache which ran into his trimmed beard. The finest soldier in Europe, unbeaten in tournament and war, Henry was also a man of culture. He was the generous patron of his clerk, Geoffrey Chaucer, and a music lover. Throughout his reign he proved himself tolerant and forgiving to all but the most bitter of his enemies and he was to prove his generosity to his friends at this the biggest parliament he was ever to summon. Two archbishops, fifteen bishops, nine abbots and priors, representing the kingdom's 50,000 clerics, sixteen dukes and earls and thirteen barons, 74 knights of the shire and 173 burgesses gathered for the pickings and the revenges of a new reign. The peers' identical robes of rich scarlet which glowed now against the grey walls of Westminster were another tribute to the taste of the discredited Richard. The nobles and prelates wore ankle-length coats and their sleeves were edged with miniver. The peers wore scarlet mantles fastened at the shoulder, the archbishops circular cloaks, miniver-lined. Rank was defined by strips of gold braid alternating with white over the right breast. A Duke wore four strips, a marquess three and a half, an earl three and a baron two. Their scarlet hoods were thrown back in clouds of white fur and the tippets in which they ended swung like tails between their legs as they walked, giving them the look of militant goblins.

Behind the peers sat the belted knights of the shires, two from each county elected by the freemen and sent to parliament by their sheriff. Behind them the burgesses, local men of wealth and power from cities all over the kingdom, who at this parliament were to begin the long tussle which would finally transfer power from the crown to the people. The knights and burgesses were a riot of colour. Their parti-coloured quilted jerkins were set with bag-pipe sleeves, tight at the wrist, billowing to their knees from the elbow and tight again at the shoulder. White embroidery sparkled on black cloth, black on white; jerkins in emerald and gold, in deep red and blue and the long, absurd points of their shoes were fastened to their waists by fine gold chains.

At the king's side sat the new Archbishop of Canterbury. Archbishop and arch-plotter, Thomas Arundel had been the architect of most of the plots to depose Richard and he had shared Henry's exile. Soon he was to be rewarded with a purse of martyrdoms. In all, 28,000 of his enemies, the Lollards, were burned at the stake at his command in the years that followed.

On the steps below the king's left foot were a pair of cushions. Stuffed with wool staple, two feet high, they were the symbol of the nation's now-shaky prosperity. On one sat the new Treasurer, John Norbury, another fellow-exile of Henry's; on the other John Scarle, a one time chancery clerk who became Richard's Chancellor and was shrewdly retained by Henry. At the king's right foot, fittingly, sat his 'hunting dog' Henry Percy, the 1st Earl of Northumberland and now Constable of England. He had put Henry on the throne but he was to die in an attempt to drag him from it. His cousin, the equally unattractive Earl of Westmoreland, sat next to him as Marshal.

It was a good time to be a king's favourite. Even the smaller fry of the rebellion, border barons like Lord Grey of Ruthin, could hope for advancement. When, during a recess of this parliament, Henry was crowned it was Lord Grey who carried the golden spurs without rowels before they were buckled over the king's crimson velvet slippers.

When the Coronation banquet ended Lord Grey exercised yet another profitable prerogative, the right to all the coronation table cloths and linen and such expressions of royal favour must have been welcomed by him. On the agenda of the resumed parliament was a suit for the recovery of disputed land brought against him by one of his Welsh neighbours, Owain Glyndŵr.

It was not the first time that Glyndŵr, a country gentleman of large estates, had appealed Grey to parliament in quarrels over land and on the last occasion Richard had decided in Glyndŵr's favour. But Richard was notoriously pro-Welsh; Henry, as Grey knew, had good reason to dislike the troublesome race over the border.

When Richard had been surprised by the Earl of Northumberland at Conway Castle his cousin, the Duke of Aumarle, a secret supporter of Henry, and the Royal Steward, Sir Thomas Percy, had seized Richard's baggage train. It had been their intention to present the train, which included the royal regalia, to the new king. It would have been invaluable to Henry, already short of money, for according to a contemporary source it contained '... pure silver, many a good horse of foreign breed, many a rich and sparkling precious stone, many a good mantle and whole ermine, good cloth of gold and stuff of foreign makes'.

It never reached Henry.

A chronicler records; '... the Welsh who saw their treason, opposed them here and there in companies of one or two thousand, saying "Wretched traitors you shall advance no further this way and shall surrender all the stolen jewels you are carrying away, for the king has not given them to you ..." thus were the English robbed by the Welsh. They kept back all the waggons and the harness, gold and silver and jewellery set in gold.'

Henry issued proclamations demanding the return of the royal baggage and in time much of it was recovered. But it took time. Eight years later in the manorial court of Clun a villager, Meredith Powis, was fined 12d after he had admitted 'stealing a gown and doublet from one of the men of Lord King Richard when the king last came from Ireland'. In October 1399 much of the stolen treasure was still hidden away in Wales, a state of affairs not calculated to encourage Henry to assist any Welsh suit.

On the other hand, Grey knew that his seizure of Glyndŵr land at Croesau on the moorland between Ruthin and Glyndyfrdwy had no merit in law. The land had been part of the ancient Welsh estates of Ruthin but it had long ago passed to the ancestors of Glyndŵr. Although he now held the office of Chief Marcher Grey's title was bogus. The true Marcher Lords had been appointed by successive English kings determined to create buffer states between themselves and the Welsh who offered warrior families absolute power over any frontier land they could subdue. It was an offer that the Norman families, the Fitzalans, the Gilberts, the Clares, the Mortimers and the Laceys, could not refuse. At the head of their armies, supported by the border garrisons of Chester, Shrewsbury, Hereford and Bristol, they carved out private kingdoms where they wielded ultimate power. But the first conquest of Wales put an end to this carpet-bagging and when Grey's family moved to Wales they bought their lands, peacefully, from the Crown.

Owain Glyndŵr, Grey's opponent in the appeal before parliament is as much the victim of Victorian romantic tradition as he was of Lord Grey. The bluff wild man of the hills who leapt foolhardily in and out of a succession of ballads and plays is a total distortion. The Glyndŵr of history was a cultivated courier, a patron of the arts, a lawyer, a poet of talent and a soldier with a long record of service to the crown. He was, in addition, one of the wealthiest Welshmen of his day. He was a rebel by circumstance, not by nature. At the time of his appeal Glyndŵr was a middle-aged country gentleman living quietly in retirement on his estates after a distinguished military career. By his wife Margaret, the daughter of a senior Judge of the King's Bench, he had five sons and of his five daughters, four were married to English land-owners.

As a boy he had received a thorough education in arms from his father's friend and neighbour Richard Fitzalan, the Earl of Arundel whose March of Chirkland edged like a terrier's nose between the two Glyndŵr estates at Glyndyfrdwy — 'The Glen of the Water of the Dee' — near Corwen and across the Berwyn mountains at Cynllaith Owain, near Oswestry. Owain's father, Griffith Vychan, had died when his son was still a boy but

Arundel continued to help the family with loans and when his father died Owain became a page in Fitzalan's service. It was the custom of the day for seven year old boys of good family to be enrolled on the domestic staff of a noble household. They were first employed as menials, waiting at table, pouring wine and running errands — since it was held that those who were to govern wisely must first learn to obey. In their spare time the young pages were encouraged to play war games with old lances and discarded swords and at fourteen Owain's serious military training began. The change in status was marked by a religious ceremony during which, watched by his family, Owain was given a consecrated sword and admitted esquire.

Boucicault, a Marshal of France and a contemporary of Glyndŵr's, has left a record of the training that the young esquire now embarked upon:

'... cased in armour he would practise leaping on the back of a horse; anon, to accustom himself to become long winded and enduring, he would walk and run long distances on foot, or he would practise striking numerous and forcible blows with a battle axe or mallet. In order to accustom himself to the weight of his armour, he would turn somersaults whilst clad in a complete suit of mail with the exception of his helmet, or would dance vigorously in a shirt of steel; he would place one hand on the saddle bow of a tall charger and the other on his neck and vault over him . . . He would climb up between two perpendicular walls that stood four or five feet asunder by the mere pressure of his arms and legs and would thus reach the top, even if it were as high as a tower, without resting either in the ascent or the descent.

'When he was at home, he would practise with other esquires at lance throwing and other war-like exercises, and this continually.'

Not surprising with this sort of training, Glyndŵr became a formidable soldier. As an Esquire of the Earl of Arundel he fought against Richard's interest at the Battle of Radcote Bridge where Henry, then Earl of Bolingbroke, and Arundel defeated

Richard's favourite Robert de Vere, the Earl of Oxford. National fame followed during service for the king in the Scottish War under Henry's father, John of Gaunt, in the campaign of 1383. He became a living folk hero and his exploits were turned into ballads. One describes an incident when, his lance smashed in combat, Owain used the splintered butt as a dagger, driving the Scots before him like a 'flock of goats'. A further indication of the respect in which he was held was his appearance at a Court of Chivalry convened to decide a dispute of heraldry between Robert Grosvenor of Cheshire and Lord Scrope of Bolton-in-Wensleydale. Only the cream of the warrior caste gave evidence in this trial, amongst them Owain and his brother Tudor, witnesses for the Grosvenors.

The Glyndŵr manor at Glyndyfrdwy was a sporting property. Its forests and heaths were thick with game and the Dee at Carrog, where the family's stone house stood, was the finest salmon river in North Wales. But the bulk of their fortune came from Sycharth, the second estate at Llansillin where the family lived in considerable state.

'Iolo Goch', Owain's bard and neighbour, Red Iolo Llwyd, the Lord of Llechryd in the Upper Clwyd Mountains, has left an enchanting picture of Owain's home life. Five hundred years later George Borrow translated the poem.

> 'Tis water girdled wide about
> It shows a wide and stately door
> Reached by a bridge the water o'er
> 'Tis formed of buildings coupled fair,
> Coupled is every couple there;
> Within a quadrate structure tall,
> Master the merry pleasures all.
> Co-jointly are the angles bound —
> No flaw in all the place is found.
> Structures in contact meet the eye
> Upon the hillocks top on high;
> Into each other fastened they

The form of a hard knot display.
There dwells the chief we all extoll
In timber house on lightsome knoll
Upon four wooden columns proud
Each column thick and firmly bas'd
And upon each a loft is placed;
In these four lofts which coupled stand
Repose at night the minstrel band;
Four lofts they were in pristine state
But now, partitioned, form they eight.
Tiled is the roof, on each house top
Rise smoke-ejecting chimneys up
All of one form there are nine halls
Each with nine wardrobes within its walls
With linen white as well supplied
As fairest shops in famed Cheapside
Behold that church with cross upraised
And with its windows neatly glazed.
All houses are in this comprest —
An orchard's near it of the best.
Also a park where void of fear
Feed antlered herds of fallow deer.
A warren wide my chief can boast.
Of goodly steeds a countless host.
Meads where for hay the clover grows,
Cornfields which hedges trim enclose
A mill a rushing brook upon,
And pigeon tower fram'd of stone.
A fishpond deep and dark to see
To cast nets in when need there be
Which never yet was known to lack
A plenteous store of perch and jack
Of various plumage birds abound
Herons and peacocks haunt around
What luxury doth his hall adorn
Showing of cost a sovereign scorn
His ale from Shrewsbury town he brings.

His usquebagh is drink for kings;
Bragget he keeps, bread white of look
And, bless the mark, a bustling cook
His mansion is the minstrel's home
You'll find them there whene'er you come
Of all her sex his wife's the best;
The household through her care is blest;
She's scion of a knightly tree,
She's dignified, she's kind and free
His bairns approach me, pair by pair,
Oh what a nestful of chieftains there
Here difficult it is to catch
A sight of either bolt or latch
The porters place here none will fill;
Here largesse shall be lavished still
And ne'er shall thirst or hunger rude
In Sycharth venture to intrude.
A noble leader, Cambria's knight,
The lake possesses, his by right
And in that azure water placed
The castle by each pleasure grac'd.

Significantly the palace was made of wood, in contrast to the
stone warrens inhabited by his neighbours. It was an act of ritual
submission vital to his survival. Owain was descended through
his father from the native princes of North Wales and through
his mother from the princes of the south. No-one had a greater
hereditary right to the throne of Wales but the family had recognised the military supremacy of the English during Edward I's
conquest of Wales and had surrendered their lands to the crown,
receiving them back as tenants of the king. Their royal blood
made them the obvious figures, as events were to prove, to
polarise the hostility of the Welsh and with these antecedents it
was important that the family should not be seen as a threat to
Wales's conquerors. For this as much as for any other reason
Owain the soldier had chosen to argue, rather than fight, for his

stolen land before the October parliament in 1399.

A tall and handsome man on the little evidence that is available, Owain was a man of fashion in all respects save one. The knights of the day cut their hair in a 'donkey crop' to fit beneath their helmets. For soldiers it was a practical style and, for those who wished to be taken for soldiers, a harmless conceit. Owain wore his hair long, curling outwards where it brushed his shoulders, in the style of an earlier time. Even amongst the aristocratic assembly he must have cut a striking figure as he put his case before Henry's parliament. The result was a foregone conclusion.

The parliament had been an angry one. In the trials of Richard's supporters which had preceded the Grey-Glyndŵr hearing tempers had run high. Peers, anxious to prove their loyalty to the new Royal House of Lancaster, hurled challenges at each other across the floor of the house. The presence of the king prevented bloodshed but his hot nobles were in no mood to support the claims of a Welshman against one of their own elect. Owain's case was dismissed contemptuously.

'What care we for these barefoot Welsh doggis.'

The words rang like thrown coin against the stone walls of Westminster. Only one voice counselled caution.

John Trevor, a Welsh landowner, newly confirmed as Bishop of St Asaph and Chamberlain of the strategically vital Principality of Cheshire, is an enigmatic figure. One of Richard's counsellors he had thrown himself into Henry's cause with enthusiasm. He read Richard's sentence of deposition and he was well rewarded. Henry sent him to Spain to seek the support of the Spanish court to the new rule and within a year he was to become Lieutenant of North Wales, a post so crucial in the hierarchy that his successor was the Prince of Wales himself. Yet there were indications that this apparent turn-coat retained a secret loyalty to Richard. Recent scholarship has argued that Trevor was the author of a popular account of Richard's deposition that gave the lie to the authorised Lancastrian version. Certainly at the first parliament he tried to persuade the members to find for Owain.

He warned them that if they denied Owain justice they ran the
risk of a major uprising in Wales but he was ignored and Owain
was sent home to Wales to nurse his grievances.

Ironically, the first spark of rebellion was struck not in Wales
but at the very centre of Bishop Trevor's area of responsibility,
the garrison city of Chester. The citizens there had lost more than
most by the deposition of Richard. Chester had provided the regi-
ment of archers with which Richard had terrorised his
opposition and in reward the king had declared the city a principality beyond the law of the land. As a result Chester, founded by
the Romans to police the Welsh tribes, became the wildest
outlaw town in the kingdom. Any criminal who made advowson,
an oath of fealty, to the Earl of Chester at the door of St
Werburgh's Church, was immune from the law whatever his
crime. Inevitably the city became a stronghold of cut-throats,
cattle thieves and criminals of every sort. Love Street, the aptly
named brothel district under the tower of the ancient cathedral of
St John, was a stew of every imaginable vice.

A contemporary wrote:

'Chester has long been denounced by its neighbours as a den of
robbers from which cut-throats and murderers issued on nightly
raids upon the persons and cattle of their peaceful neighbours,
claiming the immunity of the county palatine to defy the King's
Officers of Justice'.

Understandably there was little outcry from Chester's
neighbours when Henry turned his rebel army upon the town.
Adam of Usk who was with the rebels explained the reasons:

'. . . it (Chester) ceased not to molest the realm for the space of
two whole years with murders, adulteries, thefts, pillages and
other unbearable wrongs; and because it had risen up against the
said duke and against his coming, threatening to destroy him.'
Another cause was the right of exemption of that country,
'wherein the inhabitants, however criminal elsewhere and others
entangled in debts or crime were wont to be harboured, as in a
nest of wickedness; so that the whole realm cried vengeance upon
them'. Henry's army camped at Cuddington where it began
'pillaging all the country round and keeping strict watch on the

wiles of the men of Chester'. It was a full-time job for the Cestrians believed in murder on the grand scale. 'Many in neighbouring places, drinking of the poisoned cups given to them by the people of Chester, perished'.

The Captain of Richard's archers, Peirs Legh of Lyme was beheaded when he was captured in the disguise of a monk and his head fixed on a stake over the Eastgate of the city. Explained Adam: 'This Perkin who as Chief Warden of the Royal Forest of Delamere and by authority of that office had oppressed and ground down the country folk was taken in a monk's garb. And because it was said he had done many wrongs in such a disguise he deservedly passed out of the world in that dress. One thing I know, that I thought no man grieved for his death'.

This was something less than the truth. On January 10, 1400, in the market place of the city a mob of twenty-eight cutlers, masons, tailors, websters, skinners, glovers and goldsmiths gathered. Seditious speeches were made and badges of leather, paper and cloth in the shape of white harts were passed from hand to grubby hand.

The mob's first target was the castle, where they demanded that Bishop Trevor, the Chamberlain, should hand over the keys. He refused and sent out a force of men-at-arms to disperse the rioters. Baulked, the mob next marched into the town where they captured the Eastgate and took down the head of Peirs Legh from its stake. Then, behind the head, they paraded the city forcing every man they met to join their ranks. It took several days for Bishop Trevor and reinforcements from the royal army to restore peace.

The spark had been struck and across the border a whole country was waiting only the moment to burst into flame. Wales has still not recovered from the bitter years of the rebellion which followed. Even the physical scars — the burned churches, the looted towns — remained for centuries. Two hundred years later historians still talked of the ruins and wasted acres left by the rebellion. Border towns which had been wealthy centres of industry and trade were gutted. They survive today as hamlets.

The conquest by Edward I had brought some security to the

country. A brilliant school of poetry, without rival in mediæval Europe flourished under the settled government, administered largely by Welshmen, which followed in its wake. Outside the towns, which were populated by Englishmen, life changed little for the Welsh peasantry. Although Town law was the law of England, in the rest of the country justice was administered according to an ancient code framed by a Welsh King, Hywel Dda. Welsh knights were appointed to high command in the army and Welsh bowmen won victories for the English in the Hundred Years War with France. As, centuries earlier in England, the Britons and the Roman invaders had gradually fused into one culture, so might England and Wales have done. But in Wales in the fifteenth century there were men whose interest in the country was coloured by personal greed, men who saw the unsettled times as an opportunity to increase already vast estates. Such men sought by any means available to widen the breach between the English crown and its Welsh subjects, chief amongst them Lord Grey of Ruthin. Encouraged by the success of his unlawful seizure of Glyndŵr land, he set out to persuade Henry, understandably insecure, that the Welsh were not on the point of rebellion. His objective was the control of the only sizeable estate still in the hands of a Welsh family, the Glyndŵr lands, which ran along the border of his own domain and which would give him a March as extensive as those won by conquest by hereditary Marcher Lords.

There was little finesse in his methods. His aim was to persuade the king of his own loyalty and contrast it with the turbulence around him. In doing so he was perfectly ready to cast doubts on the abilities and loyalties not only of the Welsh but on those of other English land-owners who were his friends and neighbours. He had not long to wait for his opportunity.

Griffith ap Dafydd ap Griffith was an outlaw who operated from the Ceiriog Valley near Chirk. He was a troublesome neighbour and the Marcher Lords set a trap to bring him to justice. An offer of a pardon and an appointment as master forester and bailiff of the Lordship of Chirk was made to him. He was invited under safe conduct to negotiate his terms for acceptance and he set out with two men-at-arms for Oswestry. Under the terms he could not be arrested in town but his enemies had contrived a stratagem to get him to travel beyond the boundaries in which he was protected. Warned of the English plan Griffith escaped, his men riding two horses they had stolen from Lord Grey's park. To be brought into direct conflict with a powerful noble of Grey's temperament was dangerous and Griffith put his case before Grey in a letter which has survived. In it Griffith explains the offer that was made to him and continues:

'... I should have wages as much as any gentleman should have who went with him; and all this he said before my cousins and the Bishop of St Asaph and that rather than I should fail he would spend of his own gold twenty marks. Here, upon a trust, I got me two men, armoured, and horses and other armament and came to Oswestry; and on the morrow I sent to Peers Cambr the receiver of Chirk three times to tell him I was ready.

'He said I should speak no word with him and at last he said he had no wages for me and that he had all the retinue he needed; but he bade me go to Sir Richard Lakin to look whether he had need of me. I had no covenant for this but I would have gone for no wages to him only to have my charter and some living that I might dwell in peace and in rest. And this, as witnesses Sir Richard, I was ready and willing to have gone had John Wale been true. But he came privately to Sir Richard and said "Here is Gruffyd whose safe conduct only applies to Chirkland, so you may take him if you will." But a friend told me of this and I fled.

'I have heard that two of your horses were taken from your park. I know where they are but it was through no hatred of mine for your lordship that my men took them.

'I was told that you are in purpose to let your men burn and slay in any land which succours me and in which I am taken. Without doubt as many men as you slay for my sake and as many houses as you burn for my sake as many will I burn and slay for yours. And doubt not that I will have bread and ale of the best that is in your Lordship.'

It was not a diplomatic paragraph and Griffith seems to have sensed this. Incongruously he ends the letter:

'I can no more. But God keep your worshipful estate in prosperity.'

It was the opportunity Grey had wanted. His reply to Griffith is that of a man much wronged but who nonetheless is determined to maintain the lofty principles of a king's representative. It could hardly be anything else since it was written for the eyes of the Prince of Wales to whom the correspondence was sent.

'... should we be in purpose to burn and slay men and houses for your sake, or any inclined to you or any of them that had been the king's true liege men? We never were so ill-advised as to work against the king's laws which if we did were high treason; but you have had false messages and reports of us and that shall be well known to the king and all his council.

'Furthermore, as thou acknowledge by your own letters that thy men hath stolen our horses out of our park and you received them we hope that you and your men shall have all that you deserve. For we think that though John Wale has done as you certified you should not be full of wrath to us.'

From Grey's point of view it was a very satisfactory letter and this unlovely man was so pleased with himself that he could not resist ending with a macabre jest.

> But we hope we shall do you a privy thing
> A rope, a ladder and a ring.
> High on the gallows for to swing
> And this shall be your ending
> And he that made thee be there willing helping
> And we on our behalf shall be well willing

When he sent the correspondence to young Prince Henry in Chester Castle Grey wrote a covering letter:

'... there be many officers of the king and the Earls of the March who are kin to these rebels and until you put these officers in better governance this country of North Wales shall never have peace . . . take our liege lord's counsel and ordain other remedies than we have powers to do or else truly it will be an unruly country within a short time.'

It was no coincidence that one of the king's officers in North Wales was Owain, a tenant-in-capite to the crown for the estates which Grey coveted. As he sent off the copies of the Griffith correspondence and his own warning letter Grey must have happily counted his chickens, confident that they were about to hatch. Events hundreds of miles away were already helping the incubation.

†   †   †

Elizabeth, the daughter of George Dunbar, the Earl of the Scottish March, had been betrothed to the Duke of Rothesay, the heir to the throne of Scotland but the engagement had been broken off when the Earl of Douglas, Archibald the Grim, offered a larger dowry with his own daughter Margaret. Incensed, Dunbar made secret treaties to come over to the English and Henry raised an army to meet him at Newcastle-on-Tyne.

By the end of the fourteenth century the feudal levy by which armies were recruited had been largely superceded by paid soldiers but a duty still lay on the nobles to attend the king at his wars. As a royal tenant Owain Glyndŵr held his lands only so long as he honoured this contract. Failure to fight with the king would result in the automatic forfeit of his estates.

Events had put Lord Grey in control of a situation in which he could totally discredit his neighbour. As Chief Marcher Lord Grey received the king's summons to arms and it was his duty to promulgate it amongst the nobility of North Wales. By something more than coincidence the summons to Owain Glyndŵr did not arrive at his manor until the North Wales contingent was ready to march. It was impossible in the time to raise the number of men-at-arms it was his duty to provide and the North Wales force, with Lord Grey at its head, rode off without him.

Owain's ability as a fighting knight in campaigns against the Scots had already been established. His local knowledge would have been invaluable to the crown and his absence must have appeared to the king as the most outrageous dereliction of duty. When the Scottish campaign ended in humiliating failure scapegoats were necessary. To Grey's delight he and Lord Talbot were given leave to proceed against Owain and bring him to justice.

There are no written accounts of this expedition by the two lords but there is a local tradition which has the ring of truth. On his own land, surrounded by his tenantry and local gentry who could be counted upon to aid him, a frontal attack was out of the question. Owain would escape long before the English force could overcome the opposition. It was essential to Grey's plan that Owain should be taken prisoner and removed from Wales. Once again the friar-clerks were summoned and a letter was dictated to Glyndŵr. In it Grey suggested that he should visit his neighbour in order that they could resolve the difficulties which were now threatening Glyndŵr. Owain agreed to receive him but he made a condition which suggests that he placed little trust in his neighbour. Grey would be welcome but he must be attended by no more than thirty of his followers. Grey, attended by the thirty, set off across country to Owain's manor house at Glyndyfrdwy. Some time later a second heavily armed party of men-at-arms rode off along the path their master had taken and dispersed quietly into the thick woodland which surrounded the Glyndŵr manor.

Owain and Grey met at the door of the manor house and went inside. Luckily Red Iolo, the bard, saw the second party in the woods as they moved over the water meadows which surrounded the house. The problem was to warn Owain of his danger without disclosing to Lord Grey that his men had been seen. According to tradition Iolo Goch did this in verse. Grey, though familiar with colloquial Welsh, was no scholar. The intricacies of the *englyn*, a complex bardic verse form, would have been beyond his comprehension and Iolo used it to warn Owain.

The *englyn* which Iolo chose commemorated the death of a lord of Denbigh, a brother of Prince Llewellyn. After his execution at Shrewsbury his heart was thrown onto a fire but it leapt away from the flames and knocked out the eye of his executioner.

Sang Iolo:

> Think on Leweni's chief nor slight
> The murder of the Christmas night
> The blazing hearth in 'Mwythig's keep
> The burning heart's avenging leap.

Owain left the room in which the negotiations were being conducted and when Grey's men-at-arms launched their attack on the house he was already clear and riding to freedom. He had escaped but there were no alternatives now. The last door to a peaceful settlement had been closed. Through one man's greed a nation was about to be plunged into a bitter rebellion from which it would never wholly recover.

II

OWAIN'S CHILDREN

ONE BY one through the stone doorway of the manor house on the banks of the Dee at Carrog passed the guests at the furtive coronation. It was September 16, 1400, and above the narrow gorge of the river the Berwyn mountains were warm with the hammered red-gold of the dying bracken. The house was set in a crook of the River Dee which forms a natural moat at the foot of a prehistoric barrow. The barrow still towers over the river and the land on which the Glyndŵr manor house was built. A top-knot of firs on its crown makes a natural observation post and commands the valley, the slopes of the Berwyn range and, in the distance, the crags of Eglwysig. It was a soldier's home in a superbly defensive position. Any movement along the valley from Corwen at the one end to the castle of Dinas Brân at the other, on either mountain slope or along the floor of the valley could be seen immediately by watchers in the firs.

The coronation was a family affair. Tudor, three years younger but uncannily like his brother Owain, was there. Only the wart under Owain's left eye distinguished them. Amongst the other guests were Owain's eldest son Griffith, a soldier like his father, his wife's brothers Griffith and Philip Hanmer, his sister's husband Robert Puleston. Howel Gyffin, the Dean of St Asaph, brought his two nephews from Powysland, Evan Fychan and Griffith ap Evan. From Powys, too, came Madog ap Evan ab Madog and a friend, John Astwick. A poet remembered only by his nickname 'Crab' came from Sycharth. A Shropshire jury which a year later investigated the rebellion described the Crab as the rebellion's 'prophet or seer'.

Glyndŵr's investiture as Prince of Wales had none of the pomp which had attended young Henry's ceremony the year before at the Palace of Westminster. Furnishings were spartan. The table was a bare wooden board on trestles, there was perhaps a bench with a tapestry thrown over it, a smaller fixed table, a chair and a long settle before an open hearth. On one side of the fire there was a stool with a cushion and on the other a rough wooden armchair. But, though the surroundings were rustic Owain's right to the title of Prince of Wales was based on firmer foundations than that of the boy who was to become his adversary. Through his father, Griffith Vychan, Owain was descended from the hereditary princes of Powys in North Wales and his mother, Helen was fifth in line of descent from Llewellyn, the last native Prince of Wales. Later in the century the Tudors were to use her sister Catherine's line to attach themselves to the ancient royal house of Britain.

The bards, disaffected and with their own power crumbling under repressive legislation, spread the news of the rising of the new prince. They and the travelling friars were amongst Owain Glyndŵr's earliest and most fervent supporters and they were powerful advocates. The fifteenth century Welsh, still deeply religious were obedient to the friars and the bards were sure of adulation wherever they went. Harps slung, on foot and donkey back, they sang the praises of the new Prince in manor halls and peasants' cottages all over the principality. The legends which were to survive for many centuries were born. Some were plagiarisms. Stories of great storms on the night of his birth, of his father's horses awash in blood to their fetlocks had already been told of the birth of another Marcher; but they did their work and not only in Wales. In London, never a man to let slip a good portent, Adam of Usk was reaping a rich harvest of omens.

'In 1400 four little bells, hanging on the four corners of the shrine of St Edward at Westminster ringing of their own accord and with more than human power miraculously sounded four times in one day, to the great awe and wonder of the brethren.'

More significant to an expatriate Welshman was the miraculous event at Builth Wells.

Llewellyn, the last ruling Welsh Prince, had been killed in 1282 by two English knights, John Gifford and Edmund Mortimer, when they surprised him, unarmed, on the banks of a stream. He was decapitated, his head washed in the stream and carried to London. In mocking fulfillment of a Welsh prophecy that Llewellyn would ride through Cheapside in a silver crown, wielding the sceptre of Britain, Edward I had the head paraded through London with a cheap silver band on its brow.

Adam noted:

'The spring wherein the head of Llewellyn ap Griffith last Prince of Wales, was washed after it was cut off, and which is in the village of Builth, ran with blood throughout a live-long day.'

The bards were efficient recruiters. Down the hill slopes to Glyndyfrdwy and along the drover's track on the valley floor young men hurried to support Glyndŵr. Some were his own tenants from Carrog and Cynllaith but among the two hundred and fifty men who were his first supporters were many who owed him no feudal allegiance. In 1854 in a Ruthin loft a searcher from the Public Records Office found an unbroken series of Court Rolls. From these, transcripts of trials over a period of 350 years, it is possible to recreate the small army which, two days after his coronation, followed its new leader in an armed raid on Lord Grey's stronghold, Ruthin.

Eleven men came from Glyndyfrdwy. From the lordship of Yale to the east of Ruthin nine more and six from Edeirnion, south of the town. There were two brothers from Corwen, two more from Bala. Eighty-one of the rebels were from the lordship of Denbigh, tenants of the Mortimer clan. From Ruthin there were eleven men and 110 more of Grey's tenants came from the neighbouring lands of Dyffryn Clwyd commanded by the Lord of Brynlluarth. These last called themselves Cewri Cadfan — 'The

Heroes of Cadfan' — after an ancient Welsh ruler of the Vale of
Clwyd. They were so proud of the part they played in the
rebellion that their descendants changed their arms to three greyhounds dormant, a reference to the Lancaster greyhound badge,
and took a new motto 'Ar Ôl Gwaith Gorphwys' (After Work
Rest). There were priests among the band and an Englishman
Hugh de Britonley. A knight, Howel ap Einion ap Howel, was
one of ten neighbouring land-owners who supported Owain.

In the Middle Ages Ruthin, twenty miles across country from
Carrog, held the largest cloth and shoe market in North East
Wales.

Its past had been bloody. Maen Huail, the lime-stone block on
which King Arthur beheaded his rival Huail, the son of Caw of
Edernion, still stands in the centre of the town. Below the castle
was the Cornmill, a red sandstone building which had been the
first garrison chapel and nearby it the mansion where the Moyle
family, millers to the castle, lived.

At the time of Glyndŵr's attack the town was preparing for its
great annual event, the St Matthew's Day Fair which was to take
place three days later. Booths lined its steep streets and drovers
herded their cattle in the fields outside the town walls.
Shepherds, their sheep draped like woollen stoles over their
shoulders, elbowed their way through the crowds of townsfolk
jostling at the gates. To visit the town was a novelty for
Welshmen. Under the laws of the day only Englishmen could live
within the walls and trade as armourers for the castle garrison,
harness makers, bakers, tailors or taverners. In the taverns the
young bloods, poets, the sons of well-to-do tradesmen, adven-
turers and thieves swaggered and boasted, watched from the door
by open-mouthed small boys. Here and there men-at-arms
lounged distinguished by their quilted jerkins, rustmarks
darkening the leather round the thongs which secured their
armour. At the bakers' booths flat loaves, both plate and food,
were stacked in precarious pillars. Geese and pork sizzled in the
communal ovens of the cook shops. Franciscans, the grey gowned
friars minor, and black, scholarly Dominicans picked their way
through the rubbish strewn streets in which rats scurried, chased

by small noisy dogs. A Welsh town in the Middle Ages must have borne a striking similarity to a Middle Eastern town of the present day.

And over all the great red castle of Ruthin. It is a genteel ruin now, over-built by a Victorian hotel but in the fifteenth century it was an impregnable fortress, though at the time of the raid it was manned only by a skeleton garrison. A fortified tower 'Erw trwm Lwyth' — 'Acre with the heavy load upon it' had stood on the castle rock before the Normans had built a stronghold there. In Grey's time the castle had two wards, east and west, separated by a dry fosse cut into the sandstone rock and linked by a wooden suspension bridge. The larger outer ward was five-sided, its Gate of Entrance flanked by two massive towers. Beneath were the dungeons where after the raid fourteen of Owain's followers waited to be hanged. There was a large well and on the North Wall Grey's baronial hall, the court of the lordships, with his private quarters and a chapel beyond it. Five more towers were connected by a boulevard, the enclosed walk beyond the battlement. The garrison was quartered in this town in wooden barrack blocks. The second, smaller ward, contained underground stables with slate roofs and stone stalls for twenty horses. A portcullis opened onto the drawbridge over the fosse. Beyond the castle to the South were Grey's orchards, and his fish ponds. Beyond again a deer park which ran to the foot of the mountains and on their slopes the oak-forest of Coedmarchan where Owain's band waited for dawn and the opening of the town gates. They were dressed in a strange assortment of war clothes. Corselets, basnetts, breastplates; much of their armour had been handed down from father to son.

The coroner's jury which investigated the raid on Ruthin accused Owain's men of carrying swords and bows and arrows. Those too poor to own orthodox weapons had sickles and, since the men of the North of Wales were predominately spearmen rather than archers, rough hewn spearshafts surmounted by narrow blades.

In the event the raid was a bloodless victory and a total success. The town was severely damaged, buildings set on fire and cattle driven off. The Coroner's jury which estimated the damage at £1,400 does not mention a single death. The records do not mention Lord Grey and it is likely that he was with the king in Scotland when Owain avenged himself on his town. But the speedy execution of the few rebels who were taken prisoner suggests his angry intervention.

In the five days that followed 'Owain's Children', the name they were given by the Welsh, embarked on a campaign of raids upon the border castle towns. In turn Denbigh, Flint, Hawarden, Holt and Rhuddlan were set ablaze and looted. Rhuddlan had a special significance for it was there that Edward I had completed his conquest of Wales.

From Rhuddlan to Flint: from Flint to Holt on the outskirts of the northern capital of Chester and then down the border to Oswestry, the 'Children' marched, burning and looting. Their final target was Welshpool, known in 1400 chauvinistically, as the 'London of Wales'. There they suffered their first defeat. Until then surprise and depleted castle garrisons had worked in their favour. At Welshpool they met determined opposition led by a professional soldier, the Sheriff Hugh Burnell. While Owain's 250 men were still at Oswestry the sheriff had sent messengers to Stafford and Warwick summoning aid and he marched at the head of the Levies of three counties to meet the rebels, on the banks of the river Vyrnwy. Heavily outnumbered, Owain's guerilla force broke and ran, to re-appear as peaceful farmers and country gentlemen, perhaps more prosperous than they had been before, in their own Lordships.

It was a pattern which was to be repeated with gloomy persistence in the years that followed. The rebels were inspired guerilla fighters, masters of the sudden attack and ambush but in set battle against trained soldiers they were less successful. They lacked the discipline and the fortitude of a professional army. More than two centuries earlier a distinguished Welsh scholar, Gerald de Barry, had noted this weakness in his countrymen.

De Barry had been sent by Henry II to accompany Baldwin, the Archbishop of Canterbury who was recruiting men for a Crusade against Saladin who had recaptured Jerusalem.

He wrote:

'The Welsh are flighty and readily undertake things which they have not the perseverance to carry out. They have little respect for oaths, and not much for the truth, and when a good opportunity occurs for attacking an enemy they regard neither truces nor treaties. In war they are very severe in the first attack, terrible by their clamour and looks, filling the air with horrid shouts and the deep tongued clamour of very long trumpets. Bold in the first onset they cannot bear a repulse, being easily thrown into confusion, as soon as they turn their backs.

'Yet though defeated and put to flight one day, they are ready to resume combat on the next, neither dejected by their loss nor by their dishonour; easier in short to overcome for a single battle than in a protracted war. Their great weakness after all lies in their internal jealousies. If they were inseparable they would be insuperable, and above all, if instead of having three princes they had but one and that a good one.'

The news of Owain's attacks reached King Henry at Northampton as he returned from his unsuccessful Scottish campaign. His advisers were inclined to minimise the importance of the Welsh uprising but the king sent instructions to the sheriffs of ten counties ordering a punitive force to march against the rebels. To secure Shrewsbury, a vital crossing point on the River Severn, Welshmen living there who refused to give securities against disloyalty were to be thrown into gaol.

The English military machine was a cumbersome vehicle but Henry drove it with panache. On September 22 he was at Coventry, the next day Lichfield and three days later he arrived in Shrewsbury with a sizeable army.

In Wales rebellion was spreading across the country. On Anglesey Owain's cousins Rhys and Gwilym Tudor, protégés of Richard II and a formidable pair, rose against the crown. Henry waited only to hang and quarter one of their kinsmen, Goronwy ap Tudor, then he and the Prince of Wales marched across the border.

The week's march to Bangor on the Menai Straits was an anti-climax. The royal forces received submissions all the way. The Abbots of Maenan, Cymer and Bardsey, the Rector of Llanllechid arrived in Bangor to assure Henry of their loyalty. Surprisingly Tudor Glyndŵr and the ubiquitous 'Crab' were amongst those who successfully sued for pardon. The short honeymoon came to a violent end at Rhos Fawr, near the castle town of Beaumaris on Anglesey. Rhys Tudor attacked the royal army and in reprisal Henry sacked the nearby Franciscan house of Llanfaes. Friars were slaughtered, driven off into the countryside or led away into captivity and Henry returned to Shrewsbury where he made his first major mistake of the campaign.

Throughout the rebellion Henry displayed great gifts of conciliation. Repeated offers of pardon were made and taken up. Only Owain himself was excepted. In the early days of the rebellion he repeatedly sought a peaceful settlement of his grievance. His aim was not to rule Wales, he sought only the return of his land at Croesau and had this request been granted his considerable gifts would have been once again at the service of the crown. With his help Henry would have ruled a peaceful Wales but there were men among Henry's advisers this would not have suited. For Lord Grey, a privy councillor now, it would have been a bitter humiliation and there was no pardon for Owain. On October 8 at Shrewsbury he was formally outlawed. His estates in North and South Wales with the royalties, knights fees, advowsons, franchises, liberties, customs, wards, marriages, reliefs, escheats, forfeitures, chases, parks, warrens and wrecks of sea passed to the king's half brother John Beaufort, the Earl of Somerset. It was an empty gift for it was many years before Beaufort was able to occupy his new estates.

Owain meanwhile had withdrawn into Snowdonia to a mountain stronghold on the shores of Lake Peris and for the moment it looked as though the rebellion was dying. The king's policy of pardoning the rebels was having considerable effect. The peasants had little to gain from a change of masters and they flocked to tender their submission to the king. Henry's policy might well have worked, but in London, far away from the spears and the pillage, a more agressive posture was being adopted by the Welsh in exile. To the exiled Welshmen in London and at the Universities of Oxford and Cambridge, to Welsh labourers who had come to England attracted by the well-paid jobs that had become available since the plague, the call of 'Hiraeth' was tantalising. Not for the last time in history those furthest from the battle were the most eager that it should be joined.

Parliament, too, was in a warlike mood. In January 1401, stirred by the border lords, the knights of the shire and the burgesses rattled wordy spears at the Welsh. In February they petitioned the crown for new statutes against them. Henry was reluctant to upset his policy of appeasement which appeared to be working well but he agreed to limit the rights of Welshmen living in England and to protect English immigrants from 'the malice of Welsh juries'. It was not enough and the Marcher Lords pressed for sterner measures. They won. Within ten days the royal decrees were strengthened to give the Marchers wider powers than even they had ever enjoyed and a full scale Welsh war became inevitable.

The uneasy peace which had lasted in Wales for over a century had been the achievement of a native administration who were the buffers between the absent English landlords and their tenantry. It was the prop which held up the whole fabric of the conquest and in one clumsy decree the English parliament knocked it away.

No Welshman, now, was allowed to become a justice, chamberlain, chancellor, seneschal, receiver, chief forester, escheater, constable of a castle or keeper of rolls. These offices were straightway to be handed over to Englishmen. The people of a district were to be held responsible for all breaches of the peace in their own neighbourhood and were to be answerable in their own person for all felonies, robberies or trespasses. Felons and evil-doers were to be handed to English justice and new taxes were to be introduced. The Welsh were ordered to meet the expenses of repairing and maintaining walls, gates and castles in North Wales, for refurnishing them and keeping them in order.

In its long history of legislative incompetence it is doubtful if parliament ever framed a less workable programme of legislation. An entire civil service was swept away and nothing was put in its place. The administration of the country was handed over to absent landlords and to Englishmen with no knowledge of Welsh, the only language of the majority of the people they were to rule. But parliament was thinking with its fists and even Welshmen who stood in high favour at court were uneasy. Adam of Usk who attended the parliament was frankly terrified by its angry mood.

'I heard debated many harsh things to be put in force against the Welsh, to wit; that they may not marry with the English, nor get them wealth nor dwell in England and many other grievous things.

'And as God knoweth me, the night before, there roused me from my sleep a voice thus sounding in my ears "the plowers plowed upon my back" etc "The Lord is righteous" etc., as in the psalms; "Many a time have they afflicted me".

'Whence, having awoke and dreading that the day should bring forth some mishap, I fearfully commended myself to the special governance of the Holy Ghost.'

Adam had cause for worry. As a student he had been involved in nationalist riots at Oxford. He recalled:

'During two whole years there was great strife between the men of the south and the men of Wales on the one side and the Northeners on the other. Whence arose broils, quarrels and oft-times loss of life. In the fifth year the Northerners were driven clear away from the university. And they laid their expulsion chiefly at my charge.

'But in the second year, in an evil hour, coming back to Oxford they gathered at night and denying us passage from our quarters by force of arms, for two days they strove eagerly against us, breaking and plundering some of the halls of our side and slaying certain of our men. Howbeit on the third day our party, bravely strengthened by the help of Merton Hall forced our adversaries shamefully to flie from the public streets, which for two days they held as a camp and to take refuge in their own quarters.

'In short we could not be quieted before many of our number had been indicted for felonious riot and amongst them I, who am now writing, was indicted as the chief leader and abettor of the Welsh, and perhaps not unrighteously. And so indicted, we were hardly acquitted being tried by jury before the king's judge.

'From that day forth I feared the king, hitherto unknown to me in his power and his laws, and I put hooks in my jaws.'

The memory of his narrow escape was with him now. He remembered the chant of the Northern students 'War, war, war. Sle, sle, sle, the Welsh doggis and their whelps' and he slept fitfully in his London house.

But far away in Wales, goaded by the new, repressive legislation it was the 'Welsh doggis' who were planning to 'Sle, sle, sle'.

III

A MATTER OF MOST EVIL PRECEDENT

EDWARD I had clasped a felon's collar of castles round the throat of Wales. At Flint, Rhuddlan, Beaumaris, Caernarvon, Criccieth and Harlech their ruins still stand. They are the finest examples of the architecture of war in Europe, built by Master James of St George, the architect of Edward's cousin, Count Philip of Savoy. The salary with which Edward lured him to England is an indication of the value that warrior king put upon him. His £54 a year was £14 higher than the salary of the Chief Justice of England and the castles he built were far in excess of the military needs of their time. Like the Norman keeps they supplanted they were symbols of power and none were more impressive than Conway on its crag at the estuary mouth. On the eve of Easter 1401, to Gwilym ap Tudor and his brother Rhys as they crouched in the wooded hills behind the castle with their rebel force from Anglesey, its capture must have seemed an impossible dream. From the East the only approach was by boat across the estuary which ran at the foot of the castle rock. The western gate was reached by a narrow stone causeway from within the guarded town walls and attack from either front would have been suicidal. The garrison itself was small. It was one of the virtues of the castle's design that the 15 men-at-arms and 60 archers which made up its complement were more than adequate for its defence. Its commander, John Massy of Puddington in Cheshire, was a professional soldier from a military family. His ancestors had fought in the Crusades and his father was one of the victims of Crécy. John had served first Richard and now Henry

and in two years he was to give his life at the battle of Shrewsbury
in a valiant effort to regain the good name which he lost at
Conway Castle.

Massy's misfortune was that he fought and lived according to
the rules of war. The Tudor's strength was that they did not. The
Welsh disregard of truces which Gerald de Barry had noticed was
never more evident than it was in the Anglesey brothers.

In the Middle Ages war was a ritual game played according to
rules laid down by the Roman Legions. It was to war itself, more
than the countries he served, that the mediæval soldier gave his
first loyalty. Fifty years earlier a turncoat English knight had
joined the Scottish army and defended a border castle against the
Black Prince. When he surrendered to the Prince the knight was
honourably treated and he dined that night at the royal table. The
next day on an inspection of the castle the Black Prince found it
had sufficient stocks of food and weapons to have held out longer
against him. He immediately ordered that the knight should be
put to death for failing in his military duty by surrendering. It was
a point of view that a traditionalist like John Massy would have
understood perfectly.

One of the most rigidly observed rules was one which had been
imposed by the church. There was to be no fighting or waging of
war on holy days: religious festivals were to be kept exclusively
for prayer. Not to have attended church on Good Friday would
have seemed the worst blasphemy to Massy. Almost his entire
garrison marched down the causeway and through the streets of
the town to the parish church the moment the bell summoned
them to prayer. Only two soldiers were left to guard the castle and
as the soldiers marched through the churchyard gate so the
Welsh rebels crept down the hill to the foot of the castle rock.

The two guards were in the barbican when one of the rebels
(dressed as a carpenter) nonchalantly made his way up the stone
steps of the causeway. His explanation was plausible and the
guards let him in. It was the last mistake of their lives. Within
minutes both lay strangled and Gwilym and forty of his men
occupied the castle whilst Rhys waited in the hills with the main
body. By the time Massy and his alarmed force had scrambled out

of the church, pushing aside terrified townsfolk, the plainsong of the monks dying on the air, the town was ablaze. Gwilym and his men had contrived to destroy half a million pounds of property and buildings before retiring to the safety of the castle. Once inside they burned all the records of the town's exchequer, a loss which the crown later estimated at a further £50,000. The bridge at the town gate was destroyed, the lodgings of the chamberlain and the splendid quarters of the King's Justiciar were gutted. Without a single casualty one of the most important royal castles in Wales had been captured by a small force of lightly armed rebels.

When the news reached Hotspur, the Chief Justice of North Wales, at Denbigh Castle he was furious. Sheriff of Flint, holder of Anglesey and Beaumaris and Keeper of the Lordship of Denbigh, Conway Castle was under his direct command. Hotspur at 35 had devoted his life to soldiering. He spent his sixteenth birthday in battle against the Scots who had given him his nickname. Idolised by his men and admired by the whole of Europe's chivalry, the capture of Conway by a rag-taggle of rebels was a humiliating blow to his pride. At the head of a mounted column of 120 men and 300 archers he galloped for Conway where Massy was outlawed on the spot, deprived of all his lands and put under house arrest.

Dispossessing the Tudors took rather longer. A month later when Hotspur left the town to accompany Prince Henry to the Sessions Court at Caernarvon the castle was still in rebel hands. From Caernarvon he sought to placate the king with an assurance that the rebel outbreak was an isolated incident in a largely peaceful country. On May 4 he wrote:

'. . . excepting those rebels who are in the castles of Conway and Rees, which is in the mountains, and whom I hope will be well chastised, if God pleases, by the forces and authorities which my redoubtable brother the Prince has sent there, as well of his counsel as of his retinue, to hold the siege before the rebels in the said castles; which siege if it can be continued until the said rebels are taken, will be a great ease and comfort to the governance of this country in time to come. And also Reverend Fathers in God and very dear Brethren, the peasantry of the said country of North Wales, that is to say the counties of Caernarvon and Merioneth, have just presented themselves before me and humbly thanked my redoubtable brother, the Prince, for his very great kindness in supplicating our lord the King for his gracious pardon, and they humbly beg for the confirmation of this under his seal, offering to give him of their own will (beside the usual dues) and without any other request, as great a sum as they gave to King Richard when he was King and Prince, as the bearer will fully declare to you.' The promise of money recalled a sore point with Hotspur. He went on: 'And you will remember how many times I have besought you for the payment of the soldiers of the king in the City of Berwick and the East Marches of England, who are in such great poverty that they cannot bear arms for the want of their pay, and for them you are supplicated to order that they be paid in manner as was promised between the Treasurer and myself at our last meeting, if better payment cannot be obtained for them. For otherwise I must come to you for the said payment, everything else being of minor importance . . .'

In the light of future events the last sentence had an ominous ring but Henry was too furious at the loss of Conway to have noticed it.

Hotspur realised that only a very long siege would defeat the rebels in the castle. His best hope lay in negotiation, in which he showed considerable skill. The Tudors were willing to treat with him but their terms were totally unacceptable to the king for Gwilym Tudor sought free pardons for his brother, himself and all their adherents. More, he wanted an undertaking that none of his men would be brought before the courts of the townsmen for damage they had done in Conway. To agree to this would have been an admission of the crown's inability to protect the English tradesmen who had set up their businesses under the guardianship of the castle. Such an admission would spread panic through every other castle town in Wales and Hotspur knew the king could never permit it. The most that he could agree was a six months' immunity to be followed by a trial by a mixed jury of Welsh and Englishmen but Gwilym rejected this. Negotiations dragged on until agreement was reached in Conway and the terms sent to the king for approval. The approval was not given.

To his son Henry wrote:

'. . . you have signified to us how that between our most dear and faithful cousins Henry de Percy and our dear and faithful Arnald Savage and others of your council, on the matters touching Rees and William ap Tudor, and other our rebels, their adherents, certain treaties have been settled; and how, and to what result the said William, Howel Vaughan and all other companions and persons who are rebels with him in the castle of Conway have finally arrived by their offer and supplication of which we have seen a copy. Considering, the good arrangement of archers, and works, which you and our said cousin have made for the siege of the said castle, giving us your advice that one hundred and twenty armed men and three hundred archers should remain employed upon the said siege, until the feast of St Michael or the feast of All Saints next coming, to the end that the said rebels might be punished according to their deserts, or that we should have at least some other treaty which should be agreeable to us and more honourable than was any one of the offers of our aforesaid rebels; the which, as seems to your sage counsel, and that of our said cousin, are not at all honourable to us, but a matter of most evil precedent, as in the letters from you and from the same our said cousin, sent to us at the present time, is more fully contained. Concerning all which matters written above you desire to know our intentions and will. You will therefore know, most dear and beloved son, that for your great pain and diligence that you have bestowed upon us for the time we very specifically render you good thanks; willing and praying you that, as the said castle was taken through the negligence of your Constable thereof, after the time you received the Principality of Wales by our gift, by the sage advice of our said cousin, and those of your council. Not to undertake a premature exploit in this behalf, saving our honour and your own, you cause to ordain that by a strong hand the said Castle may be restored into your hand. And for as seems good to the sages of our Council that this charge ought not to appertain to anyone but you, who have the said Castle and the Lordship thereof in fee; nevertheless we, considering the great charges you have sustained since the commencement of your settlement therein, and that on this account you cannot well sustain the said great charge without other aid — we will, therefore, by the assent of our said council, that you should be relieved out of our treasure . . .'

The message was clear, the king wanted blood and Hotspur and Gwilym Tudor began the disgraceful negotiations that were to provide it.

Men were not easily shocked in the late Middle Ages. The wars in France, in Scotland, and in Ireland, and the terrible mass deaths of the plague years had blunted the high chivalry of earlier centuries. But the deal for the return of Conway Castle shocked even that bloodthirsty generation.

Adam of Usk wrote:

'. . . on the 28th of May next following the Welsh surrendered the said Castle, cowardly for themselves and treacherously for their comrades. For having bound twelve of their number who were very hateful to the prince, by stealth as they slept after the night watches, they gave them up on condition of saving their own and others lives. And the nine thus bound and yielded up to the prince they straight away saw them drawn, disembowelled, hanged, beheaded, and quartered.'

It was a small victory for Hotspur but one even more disgraceful than defeat and it may have been this shabby deal which produced in him the depression obvious in his next despatch to the Council. He wrote:

'. . . the great want and necessity I saw in all the country, in good faith, are so insupportable that I cannot bear them any longer than the end of the month, or three or four days longer . . .'

Diplomacy was not an attribute of Henry's Council. At this crisis in Hotspur's affairs, his soldiers unpaid and the people around him starving, the Privy Council ordered him to use greater diligence in the care of his castles. A similar order had gone to every Marcher Lord but Hotspur obviously saw in it a personal attack. His reply was icy.

'. . . as to what is written in your said letters that I do well and safely guard all the castles which I have in keeping for the term of my life or otherwise, in the said parts, so that from my negligence no pillage, damage or other loss happen to either the castles or the country . . . I am charged upon pain of forfeiting the said castles and the profits appertaining thereto without ever having being restored or admitted to the keeping of any of them.

'I wish you to know that I have not in Wales any castle of my keeping for which I cannot answer and will not answer for.'

There remained the question of the luckless Massy whom Prince Henry was ordered to send to his father. He wrote:

'. . . certain knights and other gentlemen of the county of Cheshire came to me begging that I should hand him over to them in mainprize (bail) and that they would be his sureties whilst awaiting your gracious command. They also asked that the said John might go into your honourable service and mine so that at Conway, at the siege, he might with his strength and diligence make up for his mistakes. And there he did well and worked hard and now that the said siege is over I am sending him to you to do with him as you please.'

Henry, had he known it, was going to need all the loyal knights he could muster. From his stronghold in Snowdonia Owain Glyndŵr was recruiting an army. By now his ambitions had gone beyond personal rehabilitation as a letter to another Welsh esquire, Henry Don of Kidwelly showed:

Coronation of Richard II. French school detail. (By permission of the National Gallery.)

The funeral of Richard II, from 'Chroniques d'Angleterre', Froissart. (By permission of the British Library.)

'We inform you that we hope to be able, by God's help and yours, to deliver the Welsh people from the captivity of our English enemies who, for a long time now elapsed, have oppressed us and our ancestors. And you may know from your own perception that now their time draws to a close and because, according to God's ordinance from the beginning success turns towards us, no one need doubt that a good issue will result, unless it be lost through sloth and strife.'

Unrest spread across the country as far as Usk and Abergavenny. Adam of Usk noted:

'Certain men of the town of Usk secretly leaving the church during the service of the Passion of Our Lord entered by craft the castle and, breaking his prison, set free one John Fitz Pers, late seneschal therein, who having been accused by evil report of adultery with a certain lady, had been to all men's wonder condemned to mortal penalty by Sir Edward Charlton who was only her natural brother, and now lay naked undergoing punishment; and they gave him up, to their great delight, to the Lord Abergavenny in his castle.'

That Lord was not without troubles of his own. His villeins rose against him 'setting free at the very gallows three men condemned to death for theft, who on that same day, the Festival of the Ascension, at the will of the second Jezebel — the lady of that place, without reverence to festival or time, were to be hanged, overwhelming by a flight of arrows Sir William Lucy who had been appointed to the execution.'

It was far from the peaceful Easter that Hotspur had painted. The greatest unrest was in the heart of England itself, among the students from Wales at Oxford University strongly conscious of their Welsh identity. Glyndŵr was quick to exploit the students' mood. Emissaries led by the Dean of St Asaph, Howell Kyffin, were sent to Oxford to fan the nationalist fervour. So successful were they that by July 1402 the University was in uproar and Henry was forced to set up a commission to report on 'the treasons committed by the Welsh students in Oxford'. The Chairman of the commission was William Wilicotes, the Sheriff of Oxfordshire. Its members included two Aldermen, John Rede, Thomas Chaucer and John Couele who was the Oxford town sheriff. They were ordered to seek out the delinquent Welshmen wherever they may be and 'arrest them and put them under secure guard'.

Howell Kyffin was arrested together with Owen Conwy and David Lekebreth 'Clerks of Wales', David Peyntour, Wilfred Taylor, William Laurence of Wales, and another Welsh couple Hugo and Emmota Taylor. Howell was the most important catch. The others were given bail but he remained in the custody of the sheriff until August when they were all brought to trial in the King's Bench.

The behaviour of fifteenth century dissidents has a familiar ring. Peyntour was accused of sedition. John Lacy, a witness told the courts:

'. . . he said that our Lord the king should rule no longer and that he had seized the crown and kingdom wrongly and unjustly from him whom the Welsh consider should be king of this realm and, in the name of his future lord, he claimed possession of the said house and sat down on a bench in the said house and from the said bench he got down onto the ground and proclaimed that the soil on which he sat was his inheritance.'

Wilfred Taylor was alleged to have told a great crowd by the north gate of Oxford 'In under two years this rule would be overthrown just like pieces of chess and thus he foretold the overthrow of the kingdom and immediately left and went back into Wales and there he has remained for a quarter of a year.'

On August 5 Kyffin appeared with Owen Conwy, John Bastard, William his companion and David Lekebreth. According to the indictment 'They held many assemblies and unlawful councils for the destruction of the kingdom and the English language in support of the traitor Owain Glyndŵr'. They were accused of being partisans, helpers and collaborators of Owain

Glyndŵr in his deeds of treachery. On a separate bill of indictment Wilfred Taylor was also accused of recruiting for Owain. It was claimed he said: 'Owain Glyndŵr, the traitor to king and kingdom was quite powerful and sought to lead a rebellion against our lord and king.' Emmota Taylor was no less militant. She 'spoke many times in Oxford this year against the king saying he is not king by right, claiming she spoke from the heart and that she desired the prosperity of the traitor Owain'.

Emmota also interrupted the reading of a proclamation by Henry. When the crier had reached the customary ending 'that all enemies of the king were accursed' Emmota replied 'that all but those mentioned were accursed and the crowd was greatly roused by the great daring and insolence of the woman from Wales'.

Not to be outdone Wilfred made yet another speech near the public lavatory at the South Gate of Oxford. This time he spoke against the honour of the kingdom and exalted the power of Owain to rebel against the king.

The gravest charges were levelled against Owen Conwy and his companion William. Owen was thought sufficiently important to be brought before Henry himself a year later on charges of fomenting rebellion. He was a compatriot of Owain's and according to the evidence the son of a Lord of Wales. By the time the charges were heard Wilfred Taylor had turned king's evidence and he accused Owen of spreading dissent in Oxford.

According to Taylor he made a pact with Conwy 'that he would give him forty shillings and a horse to ride forthwith to Wales to the said Owain'. He accused Conwy 'by will, deeds and words of being a confederate and supporter of the said Owain in all his treacheries against the Lord King'.

Owen's defence was short but effective. He challenged his one-time supporter to trial by battle, a perfectly legal device. The date was fixed for November 13 but Taylor's nerve failed and he admitted he had given false evidence. Conwy was freed but in accordance with the law Taylor was hanged at Tyburn. In the event Conwy's spirited defence tactic saved all. At the subsequent trial no witnesses could be found and the conspirators were all freed. Included amongst them was Howel Kyffin who, it had been charged, was 'agent for the traitor Owain sending messages concerning the state and council of the realm to Owain with whom he is an adherent and collaborator'.

Owain's intelligence service was already highly efficient. A parson, John ap Howell of Ross on Wye, had been accused of 'riding to the traitor Owain telling him everything he had heard in the kingdom'. It was said that Parson Howell 'employed little Welsh beggar boys as agents to Owain'.

Henry's honeymoon with his people was a short one. The country was now in the hands of a military junta. More soldier than theologian the king did little to control the growing contempt his generals were showing towards the clerics and they came to regret the passing of the late king whose piety had been more obvious than that of his successor. Fostered by the middle strata of the church establishment whose riches were threatened by the soldiers in power a movement began for the rehabilitation of Richard.

Across the border in Scotland King Robert's nobles were not slow to turn this movement to advantage. A story soon spread from the Scottish court that Richard was alive. He had been found, the story went, wandering witless on a beach on the western coast of Scotland. The clansmen who found him took him, as a curiosity, to Donald, the Lord of the Isles. In Donald's kitchen his jester who had served in the English court recognised the man as Richard and the stranger was sent to the Scottish court. There the man, whoever he was, was treated as a king. The accounts of the king's brother, the Duke of Albany, have entries over four years detailing expenses for 'maintaining King Richard of England' at a total cost of £773 6s 3d, a formidable sum for the times.

An early historian, Bower, claimed that King Robert kept the king until his death when Albany on becoming Regent took him into his care. Bower further claims that Richard died in Scotland in 1419 in Stirling Castle and was buried in the church of the preaching friars in the town. Whatever the truth of the story England in 1402 was alive with it. One of the supposed king's guardians was in private correspondence with Henry IV who offered him a safe conduct through England for an interview. When later in the reign the Earl of Northumberland was forced to flee to Scotland one of his early requests was to see the supposed Richard. The request was refused.

The story of Richard's return had the effect of polarising the opposition to the new regime in England. Franciscan friars spread it as they wandered preaching through the kingdom. The king's standard would be raised in midsummer, they claimed. One friar, from Aylesbury, was questioned by the king himself.

Henry demanded: 'What would you do if Richard did come forward again?'

'I would fight for him though I had nothing but a stick in my hand,' the friar replied.

'And what would you have done with me?' the king asked.

'I would have you Duke of Lancaster.'

'You are not my friend,' said the king. 'By my head, your head shall fall.'

The campaign for Richard's return benefited the revolt in Wales. At Leicester eight Franciscans were charged with collecting money for Owain Glyndŵr. Two juries refused to have religious blood on their hands but a third proved more amenable and all eight were beheaded. Others were more fortunate. In Cambridge an aged friar was accused of uttering treasonable words by a woman and the court ruled that the question could only be settled by combat, the woman to have the use of her hands, the man to have one hand tied behind his back. But the Archbishop of Canterbury intervened and the friar went free. A Chester man, William Clark, a writer of Canterbury, was less fortunate. A supporter of Owain Glyndŵr he was 'first reft of his tongue, for that he had uttered against the king wicked words, laying them to the charge of others, and then of his right hand wherewith he had written them and lastly, by penalty of talion, because he had not made good his charges, was beheaded in the Tower'.

Even heretics joined the debate. A chaplain, Sir William Sawtre, chained to a post and standing in a barrel packed with live faggots defied the Archbishop of Canterbury. He told him as the flames were lit: 'I, sent by God declare to thee that thou and all thy clergy and the king also shall die, anon, an evil death and the tongue of a strange people shall hold sway in the land.'

Belief in Richard's return was not confined to the lower orders and the priests. Sir Roger Clarendon, a natural son of the Black Prince, was arrested trying to raise support for his half-brother. Not gifted with the martial talents of his father Sir Roger lost his trial by battle. He, his squire and his valet were all hanged.

The campaign was a tremendous boost to Owain. Funds poured into his camp from religious houses and lay supporters in England. When, eight years later, a plot to finance Owain was investigated it was alleged that eleven religious houses in England had sent him a total of half a million pounds.

The revolution made strange bed-fellows, even Owain's own family was split. Four of his daughters were married to English squires. One, Alice, later became the wife of Sir John Skydmore the deputy steward of Henry's Lordship of Brecon and an esquire to the King. In the early days of the revolution Sir John's loyalty to the crown was beyond question but his brother Philpot became one of Glyndŵr's senior captains. Philpot who had been custodian for the king of Carreg Cennen Castle in South Wales was ousted from his post by his royalist brother. Another Glyndŵr kinsman, Davy Gam, was to prove Owain's most obdurate enemy. Yet another cousin Sele of Nannau tried, as Gam was to do, to assassinate Owain. Families with long traditions of loyalty to the English crown came over to Owain. Sir Howell of the Battle Axe had been granted new arms by Edward III, those of France with a battle axe on the bend sinister, as a reward for the part he played in the capture of the French king John at the Battle of Poitiers. To commemorate his feat in the battle the Black Prince ordered 'a messe of meat' to be served daily before Sir Howell's famous battle axe until his death and afterwards to the poor. A Welsh poem in the margin of the Harleian Manuscript commemorates the award:

Place on the table my sewer
Bearing the axe which came
From the presence of the king
With blood on the edge.
The two dishes I have chosen.
The drink must be blood and water.

Sir Howell was the archetypal royalist yet his nephew, Evan ab Einion ap Gruffydd, the royal sheriff in Caernarvon, came out with Owain. Another cousin of the Welsh leader, John of Mawddwy who had married the daughter of a Shropshire land-owner was beggared by Welsh raids.

When in a subsequent assault on Caernarvon Castle a royalist, Evan ap Meredith, died in the siege, his brother Robert was among the rebels who prevented his body being taken for burial to the family vault.

Supported by the stories of Richard's return it was not only the Welsh nobles who were turning to Owain. In the papers of intelligence of the reign the following report from the Chamberlain at Caernarvon Castle is included:

'This be credence of mouth, that is to say how John Salghall, Constable of Harlech, certified and warned by letter to the Chamberlain of Caernarvon how that a gentleman of Wales that most know was with Med ap Owyn in great specialty and warned him of an accord made between the same Med and men of the Outer Isles and of Scotland, through letters in and out, as he informed him, that they should come and land and arrive at Abermouth and Eye betwixt this and Midsummer night with their power; and that the same Med should privately warn his friends to make ready horses and harness against that time; for which warning the same gentleman dare not pass from the town of Harlech. It does seem to be true because of the way the Welsh are behaving for they sell their cattle and buy horses and harness, saddles, bows and arrows. And reckless men of many counties leave their homes and thrifty governance and assemble in desolate places and wild and hold many meetings privately and though we do not know their purpose the young people are difficult to govern.'

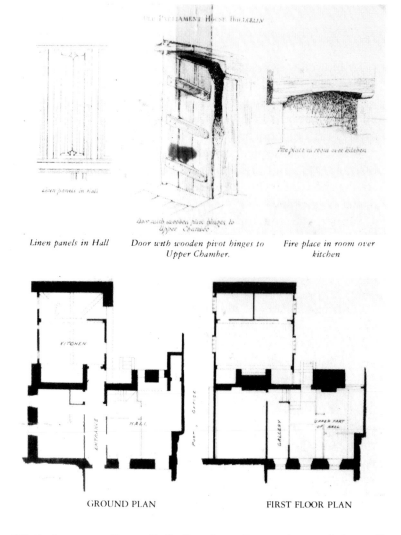

Linen panels in Hall Door with wooden pivot hinges to Upper Chamber. Fire place in room over kitchen

GROUND PLAN FIRST FLOOR PLAN

Old Parliamentary House, Dollgelly (plan). (By permission of Gwynedd Archives.)

IV

EVERY MAN SHALL HAVE WEAPONS

HOTSPUR had put a time limit on his loyalty and when it was reached he abandoned North Wales to the rebels. On May 17, 1401 he had written to the Privy Council asking for their instructions for the governance of the rebels and repeating his demands for pay for his soldiers. The reply was obviously not to his taste for on June 4 he wrote again. His letter contained news of a victory against Owain but it is plain from his tone that Hotspur had already made up his mind to return to his Scottish border estates. He wrote:

'I see much pillage and mischief in the country, that good and hasty measures ought to be immediately adopted by sea as well as by land. All the country is without doubt in great peril of being destroyed by the rebels if I should leave before the arrival of my successor, the which will be an affair of necessity; for I cannot bear the cost that I am put to without ordering from you. And touching this that has been done by my very honoured uncle and other forces in his company, I hope that it has been certified unto you and of my doing this (*illegible in manuscript*) by land and sea for my soldier's pay and my own expenses, and for the journey I had on the 13th May last to Cader Idris, God Be Praised. The bearer John Irby was with me and can acquaint you with the particulars. Monsieur Hugh Browe was with me with twelve lances and one hundred archers of my right honourable cousin the Earl of Arundel, without any other aid, at my proper charges;

and by such governance as you may see meet to order for this answer; for I do not here await your answer by the aforesaid James Strangeways of the under-mentioned and other matters; and please to know that news have reached me this day from the Sieur of Powis, as to his combat with Owen de Glyndyfrdwy, whom he hath discomfited, and wounded many of his men on his way to my much honoured uncle and myself as he certified, for which I thank God.'

Hotspur had met a marauding party of Owain's numbering 120 men-at-arms and put them to flight. As they fell back to Lake Peris the Sieur of Powis, John Charlton, had fallen upon them and inflicted a heavy defeat. Owain himself narrowly escaped capture but an important relic fell into the hands of the English. It was an ancient banner 'painted with maidens with red hands' and it had a mystic power for the Welsh. Its end was ignominious for it was made into nightshirts for King Henry and the Prince of Wales.

Hotspur ought to have pursued the advantage he had won and attacked the rebels in their mountain retreat. Instead he peremptorily threw up his command and retired with his retainers to Scotland. Two years later the king was to accuse him of making a secret treaty with Owain at this time and such facts as are known endorse this view. Later in the year it was Hotspur's father and cousin who were chosen by Glyndŵr as inter- mediaries with the king and after he retired to the borders Hotspur's Welsh squire from Denbigh Castle was the bearer of letters between the two men.

Signs of friendship between Hotspur and the king are harder to find. He refused to accept knighthood from Henry and his complaints about pay were merely a device. The royal accounts for the period show that in the first years of his reign the Percy family, father and son, received nearly half a million pounds in money and vast tracts of land from Henry. The Percys owned the Isle of Man, a great swathe of Wales and the entire March which separated England from Scotland.

Two years later when Hotspur finally broke with the king he claimed that he had only agreed to help Henry to win back his estates, not to seize the crown. He had wanted the crown to go to the lawful heir, Edmund Mortimer, the infant Earl of March, a direct descendant of Lionel, the second son of Edward III. The Earl was Hotspur's nephew.

Whatever his reasons, Hotspur's departure gave Owain time to regroup and work out a new strategy. Owain's guerillas were no match against the Crown and a new plan of campaign was vital. Confrontation invariably ended in disaster. The key to victory was in surprise. The concentration of English forces was in the North. In the still peaceful south army garrisons were less vigilant and, unlike the north, there was no restriction on movement about the country.

It was there that Owain decided to fight. Leaving a small party to defend his headquarters in Snowdonia Owain moved his main force to a forward base on Plynlimmon Mountain in the central uplands of Wales from which he could strike either into North Wales or the rich lands of the South.

The threat which he now presented was of particular significance to one powerful section of the southern population. The immigrant Flemings owed their successful colonisation of South Pembroke to the favour of the crown. Their community had spread until they occupied parts of the Gower Peninsula, coastal Carmarthenshire and South Cardiganshire. A successful native rising was the last thing that the Flemings wanted to see. Faced with the choice of fighting Owain or losing their prosperous holdings in Wales, they chose to fight. An army of 1500 Flemings was despatched to meet the Welsh rebels. Owain's much smaller force, an estimated 400 men, was camped in a mountain glen in the Hyddgen valley, twelve miles from the town of Llanidloes, when the Flemings burst in upon them. Two blocks of white quartz mark the site, two miles from the rebel H.Q. on Plynlimmon Fawr. They are still known as the Covenant Stones of Owain Glyndŵr.

Owain was trapped. Tactically he could not have been in a worse position. The Fleming army ringed the rim of the glen and their downhill charge gave them a formidable advantage over the Welsh, forced to fight uphill. Surrounded and surprised Owain's soldiers prepared for a battle which could logically end only in death or capture.

The earliest history of Owain Glyndŵr was written in the 18th century. Its source was a fifteenth century manuscript since lost but then in the Library of Jesus College, Oxford. Its compiler was the 'judicious antiquary' Robert Vaughan of Hengwrt. He described the battle:

'The Flemings whom Owain distressed most of all raised 1500 men and went against him, being full of confidence that they would either kill him or take him. They hemmed him in on all sides so that he could not possibly get off without fighting at a great disadvantage. He and his men fought manfully a great while, in their own defence, against them. Finding themselves surrounded and hard put to it, they resolved at length to make their way through or perish in the attempt; so, falling on furiously, with courage whetted with despair they put the enemy, after a sharp dispute, to confusion; and they pursued so eagerly their advantage, that they bade them give ground, and in the end to fly outright, leaving 200 of their men dead on the spot of the engagement. This victory rendered Owain considerable renown and was the means to bring many to his side, that his number was greatly increased.'

It was by any standards a magnificent victory. Against odds of terrain and numbers the Welsh had utterly routed a determined enemy. It was the spark the rebellion needed, a victory for the Welsh and a defeat for a prosperous community of foreigners. The path of Owain's 'Children' after it was marked in fire. People and houses, their broken playthings, were smashed. There was no trace now of the peaceful lawyer and the benevolent host of Sycharth. At Radnor Owain sacked the castle and beheaded the entire garrison of sixty in the outer ward. Cistercian monks fled as Owain's rebels burned down the Abbey of Cymer, in revenge no doubt for the Abbot's submission to Henry. Montgomery town was left a smouldering ruin, its streets choked with dead. Red-eyed, drunk with slaughter and looted wine the Children, anxious to avenge their earlier defeat, once again marched on Welshpool. At the English H.Q. in Chester intelligence reports charted their route:

'. . . it had been confirmed that Owain of Glendour and R de B with a great number of rebels were yday at the burial of two knights of the Lordship of C who were killed on your last journey into Wales and they lay with their host last night one league from this part of the B. Their purpose is to come and destroy my lands together with the Lordship of D and the Lordship of C, I do not know which for certain.

'For this reason, most powerful lord, may it please you to be advised in this matter by your wise council and, with their good advice and discretion, make arrangements for aid. Bearing in mind my most noble lord that I have with me only a handful of English people to make any charge upon them. Nevertheless with the people of my lands I will make it my business to resist the said rebels until greater help comes from you, most powerful lord.

'And, most honoured lord, if the rebels want to drag themselves further into South Wales or into another estate your council will have sufficient knowledge of the places where they can be found . . .'

At Welshpool, once again, the Welsh were defeated by the superior forces of Charlton but it was a dear victory. When the battle was over the town was a smoking ruin.

In London Henry, for the first time in his military career, vacillated; first ordering a new expedition into Wales and then cancelling it in the face of the penury of his treasury. In the mountains Owain was in better case. His treasury was full and despite the reversal at Welshpool his soldiers were in good heart.

Those months in the mountains were the golden time. The meadows round his camp were thick with the cattle his men had driven from the lowlands and the higher slopes white with herds of sheep. Relaxed now, the blood bath over, Owain was able once again to entertain visiting poets. The Children equally adept with the *crwth* and the axe sang to the music of harps.

Owain's five sons Griffith, Meredith, Madoc, Thomas and John were all captains in his host. His two unmarried daughters Catherine and Alice, whose subsequent alliances were to bring him powerful English allies, held court with their mother, entertaining the land-owners who, increasingly, now he was a success, came to pledge allegiance to the Glyndŵr cause. But it was a brief interlude. On September 18, financed by judicious blackmail, extortion and heavy borrowings Henry rode to Worcester and at last summoned the army with which he hoped to crush Welsh opposition. He wrote to his son, the Prince of Wales:

'. . . Owen Glendower and other rebels of our land of Wales, now recently risen against us and our majesty have assembled in great numbers and from one day to the next commit many grievances and destructive deeds against our faithful subjects there who do not wish to concur with their evil purpose.

'And by such coercion a large part of our aforesaid country has been given over to the rebels and, according to our reports, all the remaining parts of our said country and the marches will surrender to the same rebels if we are not there in person to resist their evil. So wishing, with the aid of God, to succour and support our said subjects, we have arranged for this reason to move from this our manor of K where we now are next Wednesday and go to our city of Worcester where we shall be, God Willing, next Saturday October 1.'

As he wrote Henry was surrounded by the satisfying bustle of war. The fiction that the English are a peace-loving race was centuries in the future. War was a welcome relief to the farmer's son. To him and the young townsman it offered adventure and riches. To the professional soldiers, the men-at-arms, the companies of archers and the great captains on their caparisoned horses it meant further opportunities to refine the skills of their lethal trade. The mediæval Englishman was a practised and dedicated fighting man. A Frenchman, Jean le Bell, wrote of them in 1399:

'The English have learned the arts of war so well they are the most noble and debonair fighters you could meet.'

Sir John Froissart whose experience with the Black Prince in the Hundred Years War had given him greater opportunity to study them, took a less flattering view.

'The English are men of haughty disposition, hot tempered and quickly moved to anger, difficult to pacify and bring to sweet reasonableness. They take delight in battles and slaughter. They are extremely covetous of the possessions of others and are incapable of joining in friendship or alliance with a foreign nation. They are underhand and proud. There are no more untrustworthy people under the sun than the middle classes of England.'

In Worcester that September the hot tempered and proud, the untrustworthy and the underhand prepared to indulge their love of battle and slaughter.

The burden of providing the élite troops of his own battalion fell upon Henry. Knights of the Household and Knights of the Shire had priority powers to recruit the fittest and the best fighting men and archers into this battalion. They alone wore the royal livery and they were equipped with arms from the accumulated stocks of the Great Wardrobe in the Tower of London. Henry's personal squires — there were twenty on his permanent staff and they were paid £7 a day — recruited gunners, carpenters, fletchers to make the arrow flights, bowyers, physicians, clerks, surgeons and chaplains. They recruited trumpeters and pipers too and a Master Minstrel was appointed to command them. The carpenters were sent to Bristol and the other English ports to fix fighting foc'sles to the merchant ships which were impressed in pre-navy days into wartime service. The ships were armed with cannon dragged across England from the Tower. The object of the expedition was to cow with the awe of the king's majesty. Kingship was new to Henry and the trappings still a novelty. His following included the Clerks to the Stable, the Spicery, the Poultry and the Scullery. There were master gunners from Germany and the 'stuffer of bassinets' who padded and adjusted the helmets of the favoured.

On local authorities all over England fell the responsibility of feeding the army. Down the autumn lanes to Worcester trundled carts carrying sides of salted beef, mutton and pork, oats, peas and beans. Cheese had been the staple diet of the Roman legions and they had taught the Cheshire farmers the secret of its manufacture. Now, from the 'cheese' shire, came carts with great 26 stone cheeses to feed the military heirs of the legions. The Commissariat was assembled at Worcester to be checked by the quartermasters. Bundles of tents, forges, stoves, boxes of horseshoes, nails, axes, scythes, sickles and spades were marshalled. Canvas-packed white painted bows and corded sheaves of arrows were packed in wooden tuns. There were rudimentary first-aid kits with plasters and soft linen bandages, even herbs to anaesthetise the wounded officers before operations were performed on them. The instruments of the king's music were inspected and issued; trumpets, pipes, clarions, tabors and fiddles and bows for the musicians, who were all trained archers.

The organisation of the vast assembly fell on the King's Artiller and his staff of military craftsmen in the Tower of London. Twelve days after the first summons went out the muster was held at Worcester and the work of assembling the army in its fighting formations began. Under the Captains the army was divided into battles, the forerunner of today's battalions, sub-divided into millenaires, centenaires and vintenaires. The mounted knights fought in 'lances' of four, under a generosus who commanded esquires and pages. Their weapons were the lance, the sword and the dagger and they carried small shields of wood and boiled leather.

By the fifteenth century the duty of lesser lords to fight for magnates from whom they held their land had relaxed and the Hundred Years War had seen the emergence of the mercenary. Professional soldiers contracted to supply men and to fight for a specified period, normally nine weeks. The leaders of each mercenary band held written contracts which defined the number of the men they were required to supply, the duration of their service and the country in which they would be required to fight. The contracts laid down wage rates, compensation for lost

The coronation of Henry Bolinbroke. Detail from an illustration in 'Chroniques d'Angleterre', Froissart. (By permission of the British Library.)

Archbishop Arundel preaching in the cause of Henry IV. (By permission of the British Library.)

Richard II captured at Flint Castle. A detail from Froissart's 'Chronicles'. (By permission of the British Library.)

horses, liability for transport costs and agreed divisions of
ransoms and loot. Normally the soldier gave one third of his loot
to his captain who in turn paid a third to the king, plus a third of
his own ransom and plunder.

Pay was good. An Earl received the equivalent of £38 a day, a
banneret £20, a knight £10, a man-at-arms £5, a mounted archer
£2.50, a foot archer £1.25 and a spearman 62.5 pence.

Each contract of service was written twice on a sheet of
parchment which was torn down the middle, one half going to
the contracting soldier, the other remaining with the royal clerks.
Forgeries could be detected by fitting the jagged edges of the two
pieces of parchment together. Because the edges resembled a bite
the parchment contracts were called in the army 'indentures'.

For his expedition into Wales Henry summoned the men of
twenty-two counties in the south, the midlands and the west.
They were chosen by Commissioners of Array at parades of all
able bodied men between the ages of 15 and 60.

The Statute of Winchester, framed in 1285, had defined the
Englishman's obligation to fight in defence of his home. Richard
II had endorsed the provisions of the first statute:

'Every man shall to have weapons and equipment in his house
to keep the peace in accordance with the Ancient Assize of Arms.
Namely each man between the ages of 15 and 60 shall be assessed
and sworn to arms on a scale according to the value of his lands
and chattels. Those who have lands to the value of £15, or chattels
to the value of 40 marks shall provide themselves with a hauberk,
a cap of iron, a sword, a dagger and a horse; those with lands to
the value of £10, or chattels to the value of 20 marks a hauberk of
mail, cap, sword and dagger; those with lands to the value of £5, a
parpoint (a padded jacket to parry the points of swords), cap of
iron, sword and dagger; lands to the value of between £2 and £5
sword, bow, arrows and dagger. Anyone who has lands which are
of lesser value than £2 shall be sworn to provide gisarmes (long
handled scythe-like weapons with curved blades or spikes),
daggers and other cheap weapons. Anyone else who can afford

them shall keep bows and arrows, if resident outside a forest and bows and bolts (blunt arrows) if resident within one.'

Once the men had been assembled it was the responsibility of the arrayers to arrange pay, clothing and, where desirable, horses. The men were each entitled to a bolt of flannel cloth for clothing. Although they fought in their own county without pay, beyond its borders they were entitled to wages which, by law, they received in advance. The cloth and the pay from the border of their counties to the town appointed by the king for the army muster was the responsibility of the county authorities. Only on the day of the muster did the king become responsible for their wages.

Payment in advance was not the only attraction the army offered. In return for a year in the army a criminal who gave sureties for future good behaviour was given an automatic pardon for past crimes. Thieves and murderers, outlaws of all kinds, marched in the king's ranks from Worcester. It has been estimated that up to ten per cent of the strength of a mediæval army was made up of criminals seeking pardon.

Apart from the Royal Battle only one group wore uniform. These were the archers of Chester and Flint who wore parti-coloured green and white tunics with green and white hats to shade their eyes for sighting into the sun. The archers were the *corps d'élite*. With their white painted bows, their swords and daggers at their belt and a mallet for pounding on the iron helmets of fallen knights they were a formidable force in any army. Far more lethal than the inaccurate cannon ball, the arrow was to mediæval mounted knights what, in the desert wars of the 1970's the SAM missile was to be to the tank. In the Scottish campaign of 1400 an archer boasted that he held twelve Scottish lives on his girdle. In a minute he could loose a dozen flight arrows with total accuracy at a target 250 yards away from his six foot bow. In the same minute a crossbowman could despatch only three of his iron quarrels. Archers carried twenty-four arrows in leather bags at their waist when they formed up in their battle formations. There were two kinds; long flight arrows and stubby armour-piercing sheaf arrows for short-range work.

The Ordinances of War were read by the captains from the saddles of their armoured horses, caparisoned in cloth, gay with the brightly coloured achievements of their arms. Before them on the fields outside Worcester the hobelars, the light cavalry who, like the archers wore no armour, fretted their horses to stand. Behind the hobelars and the mounted archers the great swell of the levies stood, fidgeting, the curved blades of their gisarmes flashing in the autumn sun over their heads.

'That all manner of men be obeyssant to the king and his constable and marshalls on payne of forfeiture of body and goods.

'That no man be so hardy as to touch the sacrament of god's body, nor the box nor vessell in which it is kept on pain to be drawn and hanged.

'That no man robbe holy church nor slay nor enforce no woman on pain of death nor take prisoners man nor woman of holy church but if he be armed, on pain of imprisonment.

'That no man go before, being in battle, except the king and king's quartermasters.

'Every soldier shall obey his captain and keep watch and ward under pain that his body, harness and horse be put under arrest.

'He that takes the faith of a prisoner shall have him and none other shall have him.

'Also that no man debate in the host for arms, prisoners nor lodging, nor for any other thing, so that no riot dispute nor debate be in the host, upon pain of losing horse and harness.

'No man shall make debate in the host for past hate on pain of hanging, nor cry his lord's name in the host to make a rising of the people on the same pain.

'Also that no man be so hardy to cry havoc on pain that he who is the beginner shall be deede therefore and the remnant that follow shall losse their horse and harness.

'Also that no man cry mouny nor no other unreasonable lie in the host, on payn that he be put under arrest.

'That Muster be made without fraud.'

The Ordinances were a combination of military duty, commercial expedience, religious observance and rudimentary riot control. They provided for every eventuality. Ransoms and the shares of superior officers, the slaying of other men's prisoners, the raising of banners within the host against orders were all within their scope. Heavy punishments were prescribed for assaulting an objective without a captain, for giving safe conduct without approval from the king, taking the servant of another, robbing a country woman, pillaging after a peace had been proclaimed and ransoming prisoners without licence from the Royal Household.

Their provisions were rigidly enforced. At Agincourt Henry V hanged a common soldier who ate a communion wafer. Yet in Wales in 1401 his father's punitive force managed to breach every one of the thirty-four Ordinances of War they had read to them at the muster at Worcester.

The technique of the *chevauchée* — the armed cavalry raid in depth — had been perfected by the Black Prince and used to brilliant effect in France. Its aim, coldly, was to terrorise the civilian population, to burn the crops and the homes of the non-combatants and by this means to make them force the magnates to sue for peace. To use it in Wales was a gross distortion of the military needs of the situation which faced the king. The technique had brought disaster to the abundant French countryside. In Wales, where the greater part of the population lived barely above subsistence level, these expeditions were to be cataclysmic.

Elsewhere in Europe the reduction of the population by the plague had brought comparative prosperity and the good life to the survivors. The peasantry enjoyed a standard of living they were not to reach again until the twentieth century. In good times an English peasant could eat meat or fish almost every day. There was home-produced lamb, beef, mutton, veal, geese and on fast days dried cod or salted herring. The invention of the chimney meant that a peasant could smoke his own bacon and his meals were varied with bread and cheese, pease pottage, milk in the summer and eggs from his own holding. Nor was food expensive

in the towns. In the London markets roast goose was on sale in
the communal cook shops for 7d, a rich capon in pastry was 8d,
roast pigeons 2½d each and roast finches were a penny for ten.

Customers who brought their own capons were charged only
1½d for the 'paste, fire and trouble' of the cook. But this prosperity stopped on the Welsh border. Unused to money, an
unwelcome novelty introduced by the English invaders, and taxed
and pillaged in turn, the life of the poor Welshman was
unenviable. Assaulted by the punitive attacks of the English it
became a nightmare and there is little wonder that five hundred
years later resentment still smoulders.

Owain's strength was growing but he knew the limitations of
his rebel army. He had no hope of success against the force which
now marched against him. From Wales he sent appeals for help
to England's traditional enemies, the Irish and Scottish kings. To
Robert, his one time opponent in Scotland he wrote, pointing out
their shared descent from Brutus. He went on:

'I humbly beseech you, kneeling upon my knees, that it may
please your royal majesty to send unto me a certain number of
men-at-arms who may aid me and may withstand with God's
help mine and your foes aforesaid.'

To the Irish king he pointed out the advantages of keeping
Henry occupied in Wales:

'We pray you that of your horsemen and footmen for the
succour of us and our people who now this long time are
oppressed by our said foes and yours, as well to oppose the
treacherous and deceitful will of these same, our foes, you do
despatch unto us as many as you shall conveniently and
honourably be able, saving in all things your honourable estate, as
quickly as may seem good to you, bearing in mind our sore need.
'. . . although we may be unknown to your dread person, seeing
that, most dread lord and cousin, so long as we shall be able to
wage manfully this war in our borders, as doubtless is clear to you,

you and all other chieftains of your parts of Ireland will in the meantime have welcome peace and quiet repose.'

Sadly neither letter reached its destination. The messengers were captured by Henry's force and beheaded.

†　　　　　†　　　　　†

It was raining when Henry, his Italian armour glistening, rode at the head of his host through the town gate of Worcester. It was still raining when, a fortnight later, discomfited, his fine armour hidden under a coat of pitch to prevent it from rusting, Henry led his bedraggled host through the gates of Shrewsbury. For a fortnight the army had raped and looted and when the weather permitted burned everything in its path. But as a military exercise the expedition had been in the strictest sense a wash-out. Snug in the hills the 'Children of Owain' hugged themselves with glee. One aim of Henry's host had been to terrify and to ruin and in this their expedition was appallingly successful. On a nation whose sense of family was its strongest virtue he practised the ultimate cruelty. The children of any man suspected of rebel sympathies were dragged from their parents into captivity. Hostages for the loyalty of their kin, they were forced into labour as servants of the English landed families. Crops were burned, rebellious gentry disinherited and executions were a daily spectacle.

There are indications that this form of bloody warfare was losing its appeal to the military thinkers of the day. In the 13th century Thomas Aquinas had redefined the doctrine of a 'Just War' waged against God's enemies which had been laid down by the warlike St Augustine. He had drawn a distinction between the 'just war' which was fought to redress wrong and the unjust war of 'base motif'.

Enlightened thought by the turn of the century had sought a return to the earlier ideals of the golden age of chivalry. The foremost military theorist of the day was a woman, Christine the Pisan, the widow of Charles V's secretary in Paris. In her widow-

hood in the most martial court in Europe she was surrounded by
soldiers. When she turned to writing to support her three
children war was one of the subjects she chose. Her manual 'The
Book of Fayttes of Armes and Chyualrie' was an immediate best
seller all over Europe. In 1489 it was one of the first volumes to
come off William Caxton's press but long before that there were
manuscript copies in every royal library and it was the infantry
training manual of most armies. Much of its argument was based
on the memoirs of a fifth century authority, Vegetius, whose pre-
cavalry tactics appealed to a generation finding mounted warfare
an embarrassment. Christine was concerned for 'common poor
people such as labourers, shepherds and such folk'. She wrote:

'For what reason ought they to bear the penalty of that which
they meddle not in themselves? They have not the craft of arms,
nor is it their office, nor are they called to judge of wars; and also
wars are not caused by such poor folk, but they be full sorry for it,
since they would full gladly always live in good peace and they ask
no more. So ought they then, as it seems to me, be free thereof,
like priests, religious persons and all the folk of the church,
because their estate is not to meddle in war. What worship may
this be nor what price of arms to slay and ravage them that never
bear armour and have no other office but, poor innocents, go to
plough and work on the land and keep the beasts.'

In Christine's view the valiant gentleman-at-arms 'ought to
restrain himself as much as he can and not destroy the good,
simple folk nor allow that their men should inhumanly hurt
them. For they be Christians and not Saracens. And if I have said
that mercy is due onto the one, know thou that not less is it due to
the other. So ought they hurt those who lead war and spare the
simple and peaceable of all their power'.

It was sound tactical advice and it followed the earlier policy of
Henry in the rebellion. Had Henry continued to follow these
precepts it is doubtful if the rebellion would have gained such
support in Wales but the king was set upon revenge. It was not a

motive which commended itself to the Welsh and opposition
stiffened.

Llywelyn ap Gruffydd Fychan was a wealthy land-owner from
the commote of Caeo. Adam of Usk said of him 'he was a man of
gentle birth and bountiful who yearly used sixteen tuns of wine in
his household.'

This generous toper was possessed of a strong sense of humour
as he proved when Henry pressed him into service as a guide to
the army in Wales. For two days Llywelyn led the English army a
tortuous trail over the mountains and moors of the wildest part of
Wales. In bad weather the going was indescribable but the king
pressed doggedly on in the footsteps of his guide. Behind trailed
the long, weary companies of his soldiers, bannered knights at
the head, their gay caparisons splashed with mud and their horses
stumbling. After them came the ration wagons, each one of
which had to be manhandled over boulders and freed from
swampy upland marshes. At the end of this exhausted crocodile
came the foot-soldiers trudging wearily and cursing the appalling
terrain. At last Llywelyn halted and sought an audience which the
king grumpily consented to give. It did nothing to improve his
temper.

Said Llywelyn: 'I have two sons serving with Glyndŵr and I
will on no account reveal his counsels which will prove so penal
to you.'

They were brave words and they cost Llywelyn his life. The
king watched when Llywelyn was drawn to the gallows in
Llandovery market place. He was hanged, beheaded, quartered
and his salted remains were sent to other Welsh towns as a
warning.

Owain and the Children were miles away. While the king led
his army through South Wales the rebels were plundering the
North. But from time to time parties were detached to harry the
lost and bewildered English army. On one such attack the arms,
horses and tents of the young Prince of Wales were cut out of the
baggage train under the noses of the soldiers and borne off into
the hills.

In reprisal the king embarked on a blasphemy which in recol-
lection ravaged his conscience. Ystrad-fflur, Plain of Flowers, in
central Wales is one of the holiest places in the country. The great
Cistercian House of Strata Florida on the bank of the River Teifi
was to Wales what Westminster Abbey was to the English. It had
been built by The Lord Rhys in 1164 and eleven Welsh princes
were buried there. The royal army swept down in vindictive fury
on the graceful buildings of the monastery. Though he later
rebuilt the ruin, there was no mercy in Henry that day. The abbey
was plundered and the buildings over-run. Sacred vessels were
stolen and those monks who were not killed were taken captive.
At Henry's order the knights stabled their horses at the high altar
while they caroused on abbey wines. After two debauched, blood-
stained days the soldiers demolished what remained of the abbey
and left it a smoking ruin on a plain of broken flowers.

Inevitably the royal army's stretched supply lines broke down
and the land over which the soldiers marched could not support
them. Nor was it just the army which had to be fed. There were
camp followers, cooks, taverners and the mobile brothels
following the host. The column Henry led back to Shrewsbury
was a half starved mockery of the glittering host which had
marched out of Worcester. Its only trophies were a thousand
frightened Welsh children, and a murmur of angry monks. It left
behind a wasted and ravaged land, a smouldering ruin of churches
and homes and a race angry for revenge. Burning resentment and
the failure of the campaign to smoke him out were weapons of
psychological warfare which Glyndŵr did not fail to use to turn to
his advantage. But his first move was a mistake.

To attack Caernarvon Castle with inadequate forces was
unwise. To do so without a detailed reconnaissance was folly.
Winter was drawing on and the conditions favoured the guerillas
but the most cursory intelligence probes would have revealed not
only that the garrison had been reinforced under a very able commander, John Bolde, but that the residents of this most English of
towns in Wales were violently anti-rebel. When in early
November the newly reinforced garrison charged out to meet
Owain's attack they were joined by hundreds of angry townsmen.

In the hard fighting which followed 300 rebels were killed and the survivors fled in humiliating defeat.

As a guerilla Owain was invincible but he was shrewd enough to realise that his forces were inadequate against professional soldiers of the castle garrisons. He was not a young man and he resolved to make one final effort to come to peace with Henry. The instrument he chose was Henry's close ally, the Earl of Northumberland. The Earl lost no time in passing on Owain's offer of submission to the Prince of Wales in his winter quarters in Chester Castle.

'May it please you to know,' the Earl wrote, 'that envoys have come from Owen Glendower telling me that the said Owen wishes to parley with representatives of my people, upon which I sent him to know his intent saying that if he would submit without conditions to the mercy of our Lord the King, I would make it my task to beg for his life, without promising him anything. He has replied that he dare not come for anything to England because he has heard that the commons of England have slain some great lords against the wishes of the king our lord without being brought to justice. And he made other demands and requests of no consequence.'

That Owain was still a threat was obvious from the rest of the letter which was given up to military planning.

'I suggest that the Castle of Pole would make a good garrison, that Sir Edmund Mortimer and the foot soldiers from this country could reach it on a good route into North Wales and at the same time your garrisons of Chester and Harlech would make another good route for entering different parts. I suggest that I with the people of this country should come towards the borders of North Wales. Mortimer should be informed and one group should meet the other at a chosen spot. It seems to me that this would be one way of dealing with your enemies.'

At first it seemed that the Privy Council favoured peace. A minute of its November meeting read: 'To know the king's mind about a treaty with Glendour to return to his allegiance.'

The conditions which Glyndŵr made were not unreasonable. He asked only that his life be spared and his property returned to him and there are indications that Henry was prepared to agree. The Earl was given powers to treat and a meeting was arranged between Glyndŵr and the Earl's kinsman Edmund Mortimer.

Had Owain's move been successful, much suffering would have been avoided in both England and Wales: the English crown, it could be argued, would have been spared the humiliation of near bankruptcy; Henry IV would undoubtedly have lived longer to enjoy his reign; and Wales would not have suffered such centuries of poverty. Such are the discourses of history. Unfortunately the restitution of his estates did not suit Beaufort, who now possessed them, nor Lord Grey, a privy councillor, and their vested interests carried the day. The Council ruled 'it neither was nor could be honourable and befitting the king's majesty to remit such a malefactor his offence'.

One faction of the council, and one can see the grey hand of Ruthin in this, was in favour of using the negotiations as a lure to capture and murder Owain. To his credit the Earl, who it must be said had not demurred at the murder of a king, refused to take part in such a dishonourable plot. He told the council:

'It is not in keeping with my rank to use the oath of fealty as a means of deception.'

Whatever hopes there had been of peace were lost now. In Wales the Children went riding, and from London Henry set about strengthening the garrisons of his castles. Hotspur's uncle, the Earl of Worcester, was appointed Royal Lieutenant in South Wales. Sir John Oldcastle, despite the Lollard views which in the end cost him his life, was sent to garrison Builth Wells with a force of twenty men-at-arms and forty archers and the Bishop of St David's, Guy de Mona, was put in command of the defences of Carmarthen, Llandovery and Brecon. Owain's old foe John Charlton had died and the guardianship of his castle went to his brother Edward. Aberystwyth, Brecon, Llandovery and Pains-castle were put on a war footing by Richard Beauchamp, the Earl of Warwick. Yet the king had not entirely abandoned his policy of conciliation. The people of Cardigan were allowed to buy back the lands of which the king had dispossessed them and the ban on speaking Welsh in the country was lifted. Loyal land-owners, one of them a kinsman of Owain were granted new estates to cement their loyalty.

All over the country the royal invaders and the rebels were making their preparations. Wales had become an armed camp.

V

AN EFFUSION OF BLOOD

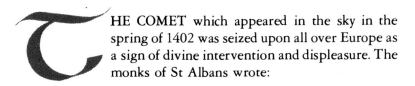HE COMET which appeared in the sky in the spring of 1402 was seized upon all over Europe as a sign of divine intervention and displeasure. The monks of St Albans wrote:

'In the third year of King Henry's reign there was a star seen in the firmament that showed itself throughout all the world for diverse tokenings that should befall soon after, the which star was named and called by the clergy *Stella Comata*.'

A century later Holinshead in the history from which Shakespeare was to take the material for his plays of kings saw with the clarity of hindsight what those 'diverse tokenings' were:

'In the month of March appeared a blazing star first between the east part of the firmament and the north flashing forth fire and flame round about it and lastly shooting forth fiery beams towards the North, forshowing as it was the great effusion of blood that followed about parts of Wales and Northumberland.'

Tales of the manifestation of evil spirits abounded. At Banbury in Essex lightning struck the top of the parish church during divine service, destroying half the chancel. The alarmed congregation reported that the devil, dressed as a Franciscan friar, had entered the church 'capering and playing his part like the devil indeed'. The infernal friar jumped over the altar three times from right to left, turned black in the face and rushed out of the church between a parishioner's legs leaving a smell of sulphur. The parishioner's feet, legs and thighs were said to have turned quite black from the smoke.

At All Saints in Hertford a month later an evil spirit, equally athletic, climbed a ladder to the clock tower where it tore and twisted the left side of the scale leaving teeth marks like those of a lion or bear, and smashed the wheels before it crashed through a large beam in the belfry.

Inevitably, Adam of Usk saw *two* comets. It was celestial compensation for the hard times which had befallen him.

Henry's reign had opened like a bright summer's day for the Welsh lawyer. He had the king's ear and he was the protégé of one of the most powerful men in the land, Thomas Arundel, the Archbishop of Canterbury. This terrifying prelate seems to have warmed to Adam to such a degree that he had early hopes of a bishopric and benefices showered upon him. Yet in November 1400, attended somewhat surprisingly by two servants, Edward Usk and Richard Edwyn, Adam turned foot-pad. The three men had lain in wait at Westminster for a man, Walter Jakes, of whom nothing more is known. When Jakes rode by, Adam and his domestic staff set upon him. They beat him and took his horse, his saddle, a bridle valued at £5 and they robbed him of fourteen marks. All three were indicted before the king's justices as common foot-pads but powerful friends must have been at work on Adam's behalf for there is no record that he was punished for his crime.

Two years later, smarting with the injustice of it all, after providing two securities of £40 he was allowed to leave Britain for Rome and benefices new. But he was out of favour and he had to swear not to do or say anything on his journey which might reflect on the king, the laws or the customs of England. Increasingly Adam's *Chronicle* became a recital of woe. Though he gives no hint of his lapse, he prays as he leaves England:

'Make of me an example of goodness that they who come near

me may behold and be astonished because thou Lord has holpen me and comforted me.'

Even for the Lord this proved too formidable an undertaking as Adam's subsequent career was to show. It may be that the vision that he was vouchsafed on the road to Pisa was some sort of divine consolation prize. Predictably Adam made the most of it:

'I beheld a dreadful comet which went before the sun, a terror to the world — to the clergy which is the sun thereof and to the knighthood which is its moon — which forecast the death of the Duke of Milan, as it soon after came to pass. His dreaded arms too, a serpent azure swallowing a naked man, gules on a field argent, were then oft-times in the air.'

In Wales the comet was seized upon as a portent with a very plain message. Hedging dangerously on blasphemy, the bards likened the comet to the star which had heralded the birth of Christ. They recalled, too, the comet which had appeared at the birth of the great Welsh hero King Arthur. Certainly it was a lucky star for Owain; scarcely had its fiery tail died before he achieved a victory which must have given him tremendous personal satisfaction.

He captured Lord Grey of Ruthin.

Although every poet and chronicler of the period hailed the event with glee, sadly none have described the detail. Local tradition is less reticent. Grey, it is said, was provoked by a second raid on Ruthin to charge out of his castle at the head of a small party of men-at-arms. So anxious was he to capture his neighbour, Owain, that he pursued the retreating Welsh dangerously far into the forest of Coedmarchan behind his Red Castle. Waiting, hidden by the oaks, lay a second party of rebels and Grey rode into an ambush. It is even suggested that Grey's own soldiers had been bribed to betray him. Whatever the truth Grey soon found himself the centre of a ring of spear-points.

It is a delight to picture the ride to the Carrog stronghold with the discomfited Marcher purpling in his saddle, his arms bound behind him and his horse surrounded by capering, jeering rebels. More than any single man the guilt for the holocaust which for fifteen years battered and wrecked Wales must be laid at the door of Lord Grey of Ruthin.

By local tradition Owain's prison house in which the Marcher Lord was confined for over a year was at Llansanffraid. The antiquarian and topographer Thomas Pennant who saw it in the late eighteenth century has left a detailed description. Grey's cell was a room thirteen feet square and ten-and-a-half feet high. Its walls comprised horizontal oak beams intersected by upright planks four inches apart, joined by iron cross bars. The roof was a series of rough wooden planks. It sounds suspiciously like a shippon.

The news of Grey's ignominious capture caused consternation among his fellow members of the Privy Council. A commission of nobles was formed to undertake the negotiations for his ransom. Its members were all friends of the imprisoned Chief Marcher and included Sir William de Roos, Sir Richard de Grey, Sir William de Willoughby, Sir William de Zouche, Sir Hugh Hals and six others. The Welsh terms were stiff. Owain demanded the colossal ransom of 10,000 marks, of which 6,000 were to be paid within a month. Grey's eldest son was to replace his father in prison as surety for the balance. On Grey's behalf the Bishop of London was granted power of attorney to raise the money by the sale of one of the Grey estates in England, his manor at Hartleigh in Kent. Even the poverty-stricken king chipped in to save his old crony. Grey was excused for six years from paying to the crown a third of the rental of his Irish holdings, which was the tax exacted on absent landlords.

Despite this concession the swingeing ransom crippled Grey for years to come. Hotspur's librarian Hardyng, the rhyming chronicler, wrote:

Soon after was the same Lord Greye in field,
Fighting, taken and holden prisoner,
By Owayne, so that him in prison helde,
Till his ransome was made and finance
Ten thousand mark and full paid were dear
For which he was so poor then all his life
That no power he had to war nor strike.

Finally, in the custom of the day, Grey was required to swear never to take up arms against Glyndŵr for the rest of his life.

The story went the rounds of Europe. In Rome Adam of Usk, now lucratively in Vatican employ, heard an embellished version.

'The Lord Grey of Ruthin being taken prisoner by the said Owen with the slaughter of two thousand of his men was shut up in prison; but he was set free on payment of sixteen thousand pounds in gold.'

Owain's Children celebrated their feat with a new series of raids in settlement of old scores. St Asaph, the see of the turncoat Bishop John Trevor, was an early target. The ancient cathedral, Trevor's palace and the house of a canon were burned to the ground. From St Asaph, burning and destroying the houses of royalists as they went, the rebels marched on Harlech Castle. This time it was only the arrival of a relief force of 400 archers and 100 men-at-arms from Chester which saved the castle from surrender. Further to alarm the king there were reports of sightings of a Scottish fleet off the coast of Caernarvon. In this new crisis Hotspur was recalled to organise defences. In Chester on the king's behalf he signed an indenture with Sir John de Pole and Sir William Stanley who undertook to provide 24 lances and 48 archers for a fourteen day tour of duty at sea. Six weeks later John de Molyngton and Thomas de Capenhurst, Wirral land-owners, were appointed respectively Governor of the city and Chief Admiral of the Fleet.

The office of Admiral of the Dee has happily survived the local government reorganisation of 1974 which severed so many links with the past. It is a courtesy title now, held by the Mayor of Chester, but in 1410 it was no sinecure. When Molyngton and Capenhurst sailed in the barge 'Trinity' from the wharf at Watergate, the Mayor and the Sheriff of Chester were required to put to sea in one of the three single masted sailing ships which made up the fleet. It was an added burden on the city. The king's first expedition in Wales had been largely provisioned at the cost of Cestrians who were required also to provide an escort of twenty archers to guard the wagons. A salted, rotting quarter of Goronwy ap Tudor which festered, flyblown on the Eastgate was the only tangible reward.

Handbridge, a fishing village on the city outskirts, had been razed so often by rebel raids, that it shared with Oswestry the new name of Burntown. The city was in a state of emergency. Owners of property valued at £20 or more were ordered to arms.

For all his apparent energy Hotspur achieved very little in practical terms. There was one certain way to beat the rebels and it had been suggested a year earlier by his father, Northumberland, to the Prince of Wales. A three-pronged attack would not defeat Owain. The central prong, 500 Chester archers and men-at-arms, had already struck at Harlech. Two supporting attacks, from Hereford into the South and from Chester round the Dee coast to Anglesey would complete the rout. There was a fleet at sea and there was no shortage of able commanders of the stamp of Charlton of Powis. Yet when in June an army marched out of Ludlow under the command of Edmund Mortimer no third column marched from Chester. The conclusion that Hotspur was not pressing his attack on the rebels is inescapable. Significantly, although the rebels were embarked on a seemingly haphazard series of raids on royalist lands in Wales — only once after Owain's meeting on Cader Idris with Hotspur were lands owned by the Mortimers or the Percies attacked. Denbigh Castle was an obvious choice for a rebel raid, yet the Mortimer headquarters was never raided, though Harlech and Caernarvon, more strongly held, were under recurring attack.

When the Mortimer forces finally fought the Welsh the battle was conducted in circumstances so suspicious that the king accused Mortimer of treachery — further widening the breach between Hotspur and the crown. The confrontation took place on Bryn Glâs, to the west of the village of Pilleth in the mountains of North East Radnorshire. Mortimer's command, a strong force of Herefordshire men, and a large detachment of Welsh archers, were marching down the narrow valley of the river Lugg when, on the slopes above them, scouts sighted a large rebel force. The rebels were commanded by Rhys Gethin 'The Fierce' of Cwm Llannerch in the Conway valley.

Mediæval battle tactics were rudimentary but it was a basic axiom that attacks were not launched on an enemy occupying higher ground. A tactical withdrawal to more favourable ground was clearly indicated. Yet Mortimer ordered an immediate charge up the slopes of Bryn Glâs.

It was of Mortimer the bards had said on the day of his birth his father's horses were found awash to their fetlocks in blood. At Bryn Glâs the prophetic vision became sickening truth. In the massacre which followed, in which the Welsh archers went over to the rebels, over 1,100 of the Herefordshire levies were slain, amongst them famous soldiers of the day who must have been astounded at Mortimer's order. Robert Whitney of Whitney Castle, Kinard de la Bere of Kinnersley, the Sheriff of Hereford and a Knight of the Shire, Walter Devereux, were all killed. Nor did the savagery end with the killing. The English survivors were beaten back from the field where their dead and wounded lay and forced to watch, powerless, whilst a horde of Welsh women fell upon the corpses and the casualties. Thomas Capgrave, a contemporary historian described the scene. He was brutally explicit.

'After the batayle ful schamefully the Walsch women cutte of mennes membris and put hem in here mouthis.'

Holinshead took his account from one written by Thomas of Walsingham who had described the battle only forty years after it had happened.

'The shameful villany used by the Welsh women towards the dead carcasses was such as honest ears would be ashamed to hear and continent tongues to speak thereof. The dead bodies might not be buried without great sums of money being given for liberty to convey them away.'

The rebel army had at last beaten a disciplined English force in open battle.

There were prisoners. Thomas Clanvow, the poet rival of Chaucer, author of the 'Cuckoo and the Nightingale' was captured in the fighting. He was honourably treated and ransomed after four months in captivity. A more valuable captive received more honourable treatment still. When in November Clanvow was released Edmund Mortimer, the son-in-law of Hotspur and uncle of the Earl of March, the rightful heir to the English throne, remained behind. A month later, in glittering state he became the husband of the last of Owain's unmarried daughters, Catherine.

Three days later Henry, at Lichfield, was told of Mortimer's defeat. Worrying despatches of troop movements in Scotland and France had already reached him and his reaction to the news from Wales was explosive. He blamed Mortimer and accused him of treachery. When Hotspur sought to raise a ransom the king forbade it. Hotspur argued that the king owed it to those who risked their lives on his account to come to their aid in times of peril. The king refused to hand over more money to the rebels to finance their campaign against him. Hotspur persisted and was accused by the king of succouring his enemies. The interview ended in anger and Hardyng's account may well be that of an eye-witness:

> Sir Henry saw no grace for Mortimer
> His wife's brother; he went away unkende
> To Berwick so, and after that came not near
> Before they met at Shrewsbury in fire.

Henry's short reign was never a peaceful one but it can never have been beset by more difficulties, both political and military,

than faced him in the autumn of 1402. Two of his generals had
been captured by the Welsh, one of them a senior Privy Councillor and his Chief Marcher Lord, the other the uncle of a boy whose
claim to the throne was undeniable. The Welsh campaign had
become a series of dismal reversals and all South Wales was in
Glyndŵr's hands. In turn Abergavenny, Usk, Caerleon, Newport
and Cardiff had been razed, burned and looted. English reprisals
only served to harden the resistance of the civilian population of
Wales and whole counties were now looking to Glyndŵr as their
leader. He had only to raise his golden dragon banner to attract a
stream of recruits. The king's refusal to ransom Mortimer had
widened the rift between Henry and Hotspur, by far his ablest
general as he was soon to prove. Daily the situation worsened and
the French, ever eager to exploit English difficulties, intensified
their raids on English coastal towns. French privateers harassed
English merchantmen in the Channel and on the Northern
border the Scots launched a full scale invasion of the English
March. The Scottish threat was the most serious but fortunately
for Henry it was aimed directly at Percy land. However dubious
his loyalty, self-interest would dictate Hotspur's actions now. The
French court was so torn with internal dissension that a major
invasion from across the channel was unlikely. Although it was
the ambition of the Duke of Orleans, his rival in power the Duke
of Burgundy favoured a land attack on English possessions in
Acquitaine and for the moment the King of France supported
Burgundy.

  Policing guerillas in Wales was not the sort of campaign Henry
enjoyed and his reluctance to fight there is obvious by the number
of raids instigated to placate the Marcher Lords which were
abandoned on the point of muster. Increasingly Henry spoke of
his ambition to lead a crusade and perhaps it was the climate in
Jerusalem and the flat terrain which were so attractive. Mountain
campaigns were always loaded heavily in favour of the defenders
and the weather in Wales was appalling. But he realised that a
large scale punitive campaign was vital if he was not to lose the
whole country and he decided to carry out the plan which
Northumberland had outlined the year before. The Prince of

Wales would lead an army into North Wales from Chester while
a second army under the king would strike at Central Wales from
Shrewsbury. A third army which was to subdue South Wales was
under the joint command of the Earls of Warwick, Arundel and
Stafford and it was to march from Hereford.

A Welsh traitor, William Whitiford, claimed to know all
Owain's secret strongholds and promised to bring the king face to
face with the main Welsh force.

Once again the Commissioners of Array set out and supplies
were squeezed from the burgesses of the great cities and towns.
On September 2, 1402 the three armies marched out through the
gates of Chester, Shrewsbury and Hereford. The spies went first.
Dressed as friars and countrymen it was their duty to track the
enemy and to sound out the civilian population to find those
sympathetic to the English cause. If captured, the spies were at
pains to exaggerate the size of the royal armies, a device
mediæval armies inherited from the Roman legions. After the
spies went the guides, led by William Whitiford, many of them
recruited locally and kept loyal by disproportionate rewards and
terrifying threats.

And finally the army, its pennons and standards flying on a
bristle of lances. The first companies of the long, winding column
were the hardiest and most experienced professionals. They
marched and rode in close order on permanent alert for signs of
the enemy and they were followed by the main body of the
troops. The horses of the knights were nose to crupper and the
foot-soldiers marched each in the other's steps so that the column
looked like a long moving wall. In this way it presented no gaps
into which a rebel ambush could penetrate. Next in line of march
were the baggage carts, their great wheels wobbling on rough
axles, outriders protecting them from sudden attack, and the
remainder of the army following behind. Discipline was strict,
stragglers were shoved and kicked back into the ranks and the
army moved on at a measured, uniform pace of twelve miles a
day. It did not march at night, nor at such a pace that the foot
soldiers became too tired to form battle formations on sudden
attack.

Henry had thought of everything except the weather. Scarcely had the royal soldiers set foot across the border than the skies opened and storms of rain drenched them, soaking the flannel cloth of the common men and rusting the armour and equipment of the men-at-arms. At the best of times river crossings were a nightmare to fifteenth century commanders. Two ranks of horsemen rode into the river at a point where the water was low enough for the army to pass through. The file of horsemen up-river broke the force of the water whilst those down-river rescued men and horses which were swept away by currents. Thus protected the main body of the army waded between the files. Across deeper water rudimentary bridges were thrown: poles lashed with rope and foot-boards of plank, which were carried in the baggage traih, with the long stakes which could be driven into the river bed and joined by rope handrails to assist crossings. None of these methods were of use that autumn. Rainstorms swelled the rivers. Even stone bridges were swept away, the temporary bridges of the army were useless and scores of men and animals drowned in the floodwaters which swept the baggage carts to their destruction. Soaked and bedraggled those who escaped marched on, rough leather boots sucked from the feet of the few soldiers lucky enough to possess them, by the mud underfoot. The feet and legs of the main body of the army who went barefoot were cramped and chilled to ice. Conditions worsened. Flood water washed away the banks of the Usk, the Wye and the Dee and the weary columns had to march and ride under black, lightning-torn skies. The cloaks of the foot soldiers hung about them in heavy folds of sodden cloth and the knights fought to control horses maddened with fright at thunder and bolts of lightning. Casks of ale rolled from the carts, plunging into craters of mud to be broached against rocky outcrops. At night gales carried away the tents and doused the fires round which the army slept. There was no hot food, the cooks were unable to light their stoves; sacks of drenched corn had to be abandoned so there was little bread either. The weaker troops, starving and dying of exposure fell out of the ranks to be left to the rebels who slaughtered them in the wake of the army. The king himself was almost killed when a hurricane carried away his pavilion and the massive central prop crashed down across his chest. Only his campaigning habit of sleeping in his armour saved his life. No man in the army could remember worse weather and tales of wizardry began to circulate in the ranks. Every soldier was convinced now that Owain could call up storms at will.

A contemporary chronicler wrote: 'Through art magicke as was thought, he caused much foul weather of windes, tempests, rain, snow and hail to be raised for the annoyance of the king's army, the like of which had never been seen.' Later Hardyng summed up the soldier's view in a rhyme:

> The King Henry thrice to Wales went
> In the haytime and the harvest, divers years
> In every time were mists and tempests sent
> Of weather foule that he had never power
> Glendower to know, but o'er his carriage clear
> Owen had at certain straits and passages.
> And to our hosts did full great damage
> The king had never but tempest foul and rain
> As long as he was aye in Wales' ground
> Rocks and mists, winds and storms certain
> All men trownd that witches made that stounde
> The commons, all of them on England's ground,
> Cursed his going to Wales every year
> For hay and corn were lost both infere.

In the manner of soldiers throughout history the royalist troops whiled away the bitter discomfort of their march by weaving their own mythology of the enemy general. In the same way that the Desert army in World War Two created the super-soldier myth round Rommel so, in the fifteenth century, the stories of Glyndŵr grew wilder with the telling. He had, they said, a stone spit from a raven's mouth with which he could make himself invisible. As their legs, bare or in soaking hose, sank in the plummy mud they cursed the day they joined and crossed the border into Wales.

On September 22 Henry was 'sent bootless home and weather beaten back' to his palace of Westminster whilst in Wales the body of William Whitiford was found, murdered by rebels, outside his blazing home. The largest royal force ever to march into Wales was defeated without ever once coming into fruitful contact with its enemy. As Henry sat wrapped in a fur gown, bewildered by the fury of the weather that had beaten him, before a roaring log fire in his palace he read a despatch from Hotspur which though it relieved him, as a king, must have rankled deeply in a man who was jealous of his reputation as a soldier.

A Scots army, slowed by herds of stolen cattle, the soldiers bowed under the weight of their loot, was making its measured way back to Scotland when Hotspur, counselled by a superb tactician, the renegade Scottish Earl of March, passed and blocked their line of march. Riding from Dunstanburgh, a Percy stronghold, Hotspur and March pitched their camp to the north of the village of Wooler on Havehope Hill overlooking the River Till. They were a formidable pair of 'jungly' soldiers, less concerned with the attractive trappings of chivalry than the business of winning wars. March, the older man, was the abler tactician. Stewart, a Scottish rhymer, sang of him:

> Whatever battle he was in,
> Victory never went from him.

Ironically it was he who was to be the architect of Hotspur's defeat and death within a year but for a moment the men were allies. Hotspur despite his name was a cautious general. He was not wasteful of his men, who adored him, and he was not often foolhardy. As a boy soldier he had been captured by the Scots and constant campaigning had sharpened a natural instinct for war.

The Scottish soldiers had first named him 'Hotspur'. Equally aptly, the soldiers in the schiltrons as the Scots battalions were called had nick-named the Earl of Douglas, their own commander on this campaign, 'Tine Man'. The name was a good deal less flattering than 'Hotspur'. In old Scots to 'tine' is to lose, and Archibald 'the Grim' Douglas was an expert at losing both men and battles.

The English army took up a position on high ground with the wind and the sun behind them and the main body of the Scots reached Wooler before its advance scouts sighted them. Douglas ordered his army to take up a position facing them on Humbleton Hill which put him temporarily on terms with the English. The army he commanded had an estimated strength of 10,000, including the flower of the Scottish nobility and a commando of French knights sent to join the Scottish invasion by Charles VI. For the moment there was an impasse as both forces, the English smaller but more disciplined, faced each other from their hill-tops. It was March's private knowledge of Douglas, a headstrong man, which decided the opening move of the English.

Under the eyes of the schiltrons five hundred mounted archers — their bows, longer and more effective than those of the Scots, slung across their backs — wheeled their horses and trotted downhill to Red Riggs field at the foot of Humbleton Hill. There, out of arrowshot they dismounted. After hobbling their horses they advanced on foot across the field until they were on the sloping ground where the hill joined the field. Unhurried, the archers moved into battle formation and drove into the ground at an angle the long pointed stakes which would impale the horses in a cavalry charge. Behind this defence-work bows were unslung and the archers, some in jerkins of leather or mail, others naked to the waist, prepared their attack. Their white painted bows made gashes against the lush green grass of the border valley. Point down into the ground round every man a dozen arrows and a sword sprouted. They placed a reserve supply of their cloth-yard shafts under their feet and beside them mallets. Armour-piercing sheaf arrows with bullet-shaped heads were laid aside for later use. Jeering at the schiltrons above them they waited for the command 'Engage the enemy'. It came from the Captain of Archers.

'Now stretch.'

The men dipped their 'shooting tabs', leather finger gloves, into horns filled with a mixture of white wax and suet and fitted the long flight arrows into their bows. Goose-feather flights stroked their cheeks as they drew back the bowstrings.

'Now strike.'

Straight as herons' necks the arrows sped on the following wind to the sharp report of the strings as they hit the bows. The massed Scots, their smaller bows useless at the range, fell in their ranks.

'Now stretch.'

'No strike.'

More Scots pitched forward. The English archer's boast that he carried twelve Scots lives at his girdle was never more true than it was at Humbleton.

'Now stretch.'

'Now strike.'

The archers' ear tips were red where the bowstrings had snagged them and their fingers were hot and tingling as they waxed their shooting tabs. The Scottish archers attempted to return the fire, but they were no match for the English bowmen. Never the most effective arm of a Scottish fighting unit, they broke and ran. In easy rhythm to the command, the arrows poured into the fleeing Scots and the dead rolled down the hill to lie, like rag dolls, caught by rocky outcrops and stacked in gullies. Inevitably the thin skin of Douglas's patience broke. Seizing a lance he summoned a hundred of his knights and prepared to take the fight into the enemy camp. At the head of a shouting mass of cavalry he charged down the hill. For three years his armourers had been preparing arrow-proof armour for him and as he fitted his lance into the rest which protruded from his breast plate he believed he was invincible. It was yet another error of judgement. By the time he reached the foot of the hill he had been wounded five times through his arrow-proof armour and had lost an eye.

As the horses of the Scottish knights bore down on them the archers retreated in good order, firing as they went, the shorter armour-piercing sheaf arrows perforating the helmets, pitting the swords and splitting the lances of the Scots. Charging knights pitched over their horses' heads in a noisy crash of armour, arrow shafts buried between the fore-legs of their mounts. It was a battle no longer; it was a rout. The remaining Scottish schiltrons broke and fled down the far side of the hill for safety, nobles and knights fleeing with them. At last Hotspur gave the order 'Banners Forward' for which his cavalry had been waiting. Turning in his saddle, arm raised and the blade of his sword flashing in the sun he pointed the weapon down the hill at the Scots as they fled across the meadowland. The cavalry had cheered wildly as each draft of arrows bought more Scots lives. Now the cheering died and was transmuted into a word, shouted and echoing in all the hills around it was the battle-cry of the Percys:

'Esperaunce'.

The slaughter was immense. As the Scottish foot soldiers fled the English knights rode them down, slaughtering them for sport. To Coldstream and the banks of the Tweed they chased the Scots until the dead lay in hundreds across the fields to the River Tweed. Five hundred more were drowned as the English knights, eyes wide with the intoxication of slaughter, watched, grinning. When at last it was over, besides the uncounted piles of commoners, four of the great Scots nobles were dead. Douglas himself, four earls, eight barons and knights of rank, thirty French knights and a host of men-at-arms were prisoners. The ransoms represented a fortune to the English captors. Hotspur's subsequent refusal to surrender hostages to the king was a violation of the military code of the day. Article 21 of the Ordinances of War stated: 'And if any man take any prisoner, at once as he is taken in the host that he bring his prisoner to his captain of master, and that upon pain of losing his part to his said captain or marshall who shall bring him within eight days to the king, constable or marshall, as soon as he goodly may, upon pain to lose his part of him to be given to him that shall give to the constable and marshall first warning thereof'.

Article 23 further provides:

'That no man give safe conduct to prisoner nor licence to any enemy to come or go from the host upon pain of forfeiting all his goods to the king and his body in arrest at the king's will, except our lord and king, constable or marshall.'

By refusing, as he did, to hand over his prisoners after Humbleton Hill, Hotspur put himself beyond any hope of reconciliation with Henry. The dispute was the final blow to the alliance of Hotspur with the House of Lancaster. Even worse, was the friend it brought. From now on Hotspur had a new ally in the 'Tine Man', Archibald the Grim.

As the king digested the news of Hotspur's victory and defiance the first open alliance between Glyndŵr and the Percys had already been formed. In the winter of 1402 Hotspur's squire William Lloyd of Denbigh, was in Owain's camp conferring with Mortimer. In Spring 1403 he was in the North in the Percy camp. Meanwhile Mortimer set about winning recruits for his new father-in-law. To Sir John Greyndor, Howell Vaughan and 'all the gentles and commons of Radnor and Presteigne' he wrote from Machynlleth on December 13, 1402:

'I greet you much and make known to you that Oweyn Glyndŵr has raised a quarrel of which the object is, if King Richard be alive, to restore him to his crown; and if not that, my honoured nephew, who is the right heir to the said crown shall be king of England, and that the said Oweyn will assert his right in Wales. And I, seeing and considering that the said quarrel is good and reasonable, have consented to join in it, and to aid and maintain it, and by the grace of God to a good end, amen. I ardently hope and from my heart that you will support and enable me to bring this struggle of mine to a successful issue.'

VI

THE PRINCE OF PRIESTS

N MARCH 1403 a new general took the field against Owain Glyndŵr and after his first punitive raid into Wales the tide, imperceptibly at first, began to turn against the Welsh.

The new general was aggressive and totally without fear. He was resourceful, his men worshipped him and veteran generals deferred to his judgement without resentment.

He was just sixteen years old.

Henry, the Prince of Wales, Shakespeare's infinitely maligned Prince Hal, was not a handsome man but he had a commanding face with small ears, fine teeth and a dimpled chin. He was of middle height and the hair over his high, flat forehead was thick and brown. The most striking thing about him was the way his hazel eyes showed his changes of mood which could be sudden. He was vain of his appearance. His only portrait is in profile, hiding the disfiguring eye wound he received in his first year of command. When he was twelve he had carried the Curtana, the sword of justice, at his father's coronation and it was a prophetic rôle. All his short life, until he died at 35 of dysentery fighting in France, he was a just if narrow man. He was considerate and an engaging warmth emerges from his letters. A dutiful and loving son, he was still capable of engaging in a power-struggle with his father when politics demanded it. He had had no childhood and it showed. He had been a fighting soldier since he was twelve. He was priggish and he was indifferent to tournaments, hawking and hunting, the sports of other well-born youngsters of the time. But he was a formidable jumper and ran so fast that once he ran down a deer in the chase. Like his father he loved music. He played the guitar and the harp and he was a compulsive reader. He was an admirer of his father's poet-clerk Chaucer; a well-thumbed copy of *Troilus and Cressida* bearing his arms survived him.

He saw himself as a man of destiny and he relished the rôle. In his youth he had been tolerant of other men's beliefs. His closest friends, John Oldcastle, Roger Acton, John Greindor and Thomas Clanvow, the soldier poet, were all Lollards, which was the religion of many fighting men. Later, his bigotry earned him the title 'Prince of Priests' and when Oldcastle faced martyrdom, Hal did nothing to save him. Yet he was a kindly master. His letters are full of concern for the welfare of his staff. He was as impulsive as his father, but less forgiving. A noble who plotted against him early in his reign received a fair trial but it took place some time after he had been hanged.

His first solo command consisted of 1,100 men-at-arms and 3,800 archers in his headquarters at Chester Castle. Until then he had been under the eye of Hotspur and he could hardly wait for the Spring to ride out against his most able opponent, Owain Glyndŵr. Early in May, at the head of a force of cavalry, he clattered under the Bridgegate at Chester and across the stone bridge over the Dee. His soldiers were veterans of the Scotch and French wars and included the formidable Chester archers. It was a 'seek and destroy' raid undertaken to answer a provoking boast by Glyndŵr; and, aware of victualling difficulties in plundered Wales, his men-at-arms carried their provender behind them on their saddles.

The first Welsh raid was a bloody affair and the young Prince enjoyed every moment of it. When he returned he wrote a jubilant letter to his father, cocky in his teen-age pride. It gives a truer picture of him than the one that hangs in the National Gallery, painted a few years later.

'We have among other matters been lately informed that Owen de Glyndowdry has assembled his forces and those of other rebels adhering to him in great numbers; purposing to commit inroads and in case any resistance be made to him by the English, to come to battle with them, or so he vaunted to his people.

'Wherefore we took our force and marched to a place of the said Oweyn, well built, which was his principal mansion, called Sycharth, where we thought we should have found him if he had any inclination to fight in the manner he had said, but on our arrival there we found nobody; and therefore caused the whole place to be burned and several other houses near it belonging to his tenants. We then marched straight to his other place of Glendowery to seek for him there and we caused a fine lodge in his park to be destroyed by fire and laid waste all the country around. We there halted for the night and certain of our people sallied forth into the country and took a gentleman of the neighbourhood who was one of the said Oweyn's chief captains. This person offered five hundred pounds for his ransom to preserve his life and to be allowed two weeks for the purpose of raising this sum; but this offer was not accepted and he received death, as did several of his companions who were taken on the same day.

'We then proceeded to the commote of Edeyrnion in Merionethshire and there laid waste a fine and populous country; thence we went to Powys, and there being want of provender in Wales for horses we made our people carry oats with them and pursued our march.'

The letter must have been received with mixed feelings by the royal family. To destroy Owain's two principal mansions was tactically desirable but his uncle Beaufort who now owned them might well have wished for a less thorough nephew.

Prince Henry's new command was not without problems. His 'fight now pay later' army were on the point of mutiny and a fortnight after the despatch, describing the raid on Sycharth, he wrote in more sombre mood to his father.

'... our soldiers desire to know if they will be paid for the third month of the present quarter and tell us that they will not wait here unless they are soon paid their wages according to their indentures. We pray you very dearly that you will order our payment for the said month or otherwise let us know and take order promptly for the safety of these marches. For the rebels hear every day if we are paid, and they know well without payment we cannot continue and they strive to raise all the forces of North Wales and South Wales to over-ride and destroy the march and the counties adjoining thereto; and there is no resistance here, so that they can well accomplish their malice; and when our men shall have retreated from us, it is necessary that we should by all means retreat into England, there to be disgraced forever.

'At present we have very great expenses and have made all the pawning we may of our little jewels to defray them, for too our castles of Aberystwyth and Harlech are besieged and have been for a long time and we must rescue and provision them within ten days and besides defend the March around us with our third body against the entry of the rebels.'

They were hideous difficulties for a boy of sixteen to face but there was little his father could do to help him. The country was mortgaged to the hilt and the treasury was having increasing difficulty in raising loans from the rich magnates. As Owain's grip on Wales tightened the £6,000,000-a-year in taxes which the country had been paying to the crown became impossible to collect and the expenses of the royal raids into Wales were formidable. It has been estimated that it cost £100,000 a month at present values to keep a mediæval force of 2,500 in the field. The pressures on the Prince mounted daily and his patience wore thin. Later that summer a treasury official received this furious letter:

'Know you that it is a great wonder to us that you, knowing the great costs we have recently incurred and the money we need to sustain our campaign from day to day and knowing how we have written to you for money telling you of our need because of the said costs and every time we have been sent nothing. Though,

according to our information, you have already received £200 of
the £1,000 assignment that was granted to us by the king towards our present expenses in Wales and for various other issues
in your office, so we wish and command you to send by this
courier all the money we have on hand at present that belongs to
us or that you can raise on secured loan for our said costs.

'And leave no stone unturned if you desire our honour and
well-being. For if we do not get money soon to support our
government and protect our country of Wales against the evils of
the rebels, our said country is liable to be lost before many days.'

The Prince's mood was shared by all the senior officers in the
army and what remained of the civilian administration. At this
time more than any other during the rebellion Owain had the
English at his mercy. If the Welsh leaders had been capable of
strategical appreciation there is no doubt that Owain would have
conquered. But the satisfaction of avenging private feuds was
more appealing to them than more abstract considerations of
strategy. At a time when every rebel should have been supporting
Hotspur, the Welsh embarked on a series of brilliant, successful
and quite useless guerilla raids. A series of letters from senior
officers of the crown have survived. The panic these raids
inspired amongst senior commanders and civil administrators
shows how dispirited and ineffective the royal army in Wales had
become.

The Welsh offensive began on July 1 with a fierce attack on
Brecon Castle. The raiders were beaten off with difficulty by the
Constable John Bodenham and a large body of troops from
Herefordshire. Rebel losses were heavy, 240 men, but the
psychological victory was theirs. All over central and southern
Wales the royal garrisons were in panic. The size of the rebel
army clearly amazed and terrified them. It was obvious that what
had been an uprising was now a full-scale war between rival
kingdoms.

After their defeat at Brecon the Welsh regrouped in the Towy
valley. Owain and two experienced commanders, Rhys the Black

of Cardigan and Rhys Gethin, arrived on July 3. They were clearly recruiting an army to join Hotspur, and when Owain raised his golden dragon banner in the Towy valley the recruits poured in. Local land-owners until now reluctant to come out in open revolt swore allegiance to Owain, among them William ap Philip, Henry Don, his son, and Rhys ap Gruffydd ap Llywelyn Foethus, the keeper of Dryslwyn Castle. This was the time when Owain should have marched to support Hotspur.

The capture of both Chester and Shrewsbury would have given the rebels mastery over the Welsh border. With a loyal Wales behind them they could have annihilated Henry's forces. Hotspur's plans for the capture of Chester were already laid and were to be successful. Had the Welsh marched on Shrewsbury they could have won the city and with it the vital river crossing of the Severn into Wales. The two armies would have been more than a match for the unpaid, unwilling soldiers of the crown who, it has been seen, were on the point of mutiny.

Instead, Owain and his army embarked on the course of action which cost him final victory. He was to have brilliant successes, to rule in state and to form alliances with great countries. This decision to fight strategically irrelevant actions may well have cost Owain his only chance of certain victory. Thereafter all that followed in the rebellion was destined to anti-climax.

The first news of the rebel army reached John Faireford, the King's Receiver in Brecon in a letter from Jenkin Hanard, the Constable of Dynevor Castle who was frankly terrified out of his wits.

'Dear Friend

'Oweyn Glyndour, Henry Don, Rhys Ddu, Rhys ap Griffiths ap Llewellyn, Rhys Gethin have won the town of Carmarthen and Wygmor, Constable of the Castle, has yielded up the castle to Oweyn who has burned the town and slain of men of the town more than fifty men and they are in purpose to be in Kidwelly and a siege has been ordered of the castle that I keep and that is a great peril for me and all that are here with me; for they have made a vow that they will kill us all; therefore I pray you that you will not boggle us but send us a warning within a short time whether we shall have any help or not; or if there be no help coming that we may steal away by night to Brecon . . .

Written in haste and dread.'

Justifiably alarmed by the tone of Havard's letter Faireford sent it to the authorities of Herefordshire with a covering letter of his own, more soldierly in tone but nevertheless alarming, for the letter made it plain that this was no isolated guerilla attack.

From Brecon, Faireford wrote:

'. . . Rees ap Griffith, of the county of Carmarthen, William ap Philip, Henry Don and his son with many of their adherents were on Monday last treasonably rising in the plain country, against the king our most sovereign Lord and have laid siege to the Castle of Dynevor with a great force of rebels. And moreover it was certified to me by Raulin Moninton and others who were in the castle of Llandovery how that Owen Glyndŵr and his false troops were at Llandovery on Tuesday and that the men there being surprised they in the said castle are assured and secured to him, and three hundred of the rebels were at their ease, lying round in siege of the same castle and at night were lodged in Llandeilo; at which time the men of the said county and of other Lordships around were also assured and sworn to him. And that this same Wednesday the same Owen, and all other rebels are on their march towards this town of Brecon for the destruction of the town, which God avert, and after they purpose to make a diversion against other parties in the March if they be not resisted . . .

'And you will know that all the Welsh nation being taken a little by surprise is adhering to this evil purpose of rebellion and they are assured thereunto, how fully, from one day to another by the support they give to it, clearly appears more openly; and I pray you, please to ordain the most speedy resistance against the rebels that you can and if any expedition of cavalry be made, be pleased to do this first in these Lordships of Brecon and Canref-Sellyf.

Henry V — artist unknown. (By permission of the National Portrait Gallery.)

Harlech Castle, as it might have appeared at the time of its completion about 1290. (Crown Copyright.)

'Written at Brecon this Wednesday afternoon and in great haste . . .'

On July 6, as Henry, unaware of the conspiracy against him, marched North to help the Percys against the Scots and Hotspur marched south towards his first objective, Chester, Glyndŵr's army of 8,240 spearmen captured Carmarthen. The town was the centre of royal power in Wales, but it was of no consequence in the great events which were shaping. Indeed under threat from a large force of Flemings mustered by Thomas Earl of Carewe, Glyndŵr soon had to abandon it, falling back first on St Clears then Laugharne Castle, a tactical error, which left him in a trap from which he subsequently found it difficult and costly to extricate himself. For the moment, though, the Welsh were content to store their vast booty from the raids and Jenkin Hanard wrote wistfully:

'They must have goods and victuals in plenty for every house about us is full of poultry and wine and honey and wheat and all manner of victuals.'

Sir John Skydmore was Constable of Carreg Cennen castle perched on a three-hundred-foot cliff near Llandeilo in the Carmarthenshire Black Mountains. Later, Sir John married Owain Glyndŵr's daughter but for the moment they were enemies. He reported:

'For as much as I say I may not spare any man from this place away from me to certify neither my king nor the lord my prince in the mischief of the countryside about, nor no man pass by anyway, hence I pray you and require you that you certify them how all Carmarthenshire, Kidwelly, Carnwaltham and Yskenyed were sworn to Owain yesterday. And he lay tonight in the castle of Drosselan with Rhys ap Griffith and there I was on truce and prayed for a safe conduct under his seal to send home my wife and her mother and her train but he would not grant me. This day he is about Carmarthen and thinks to abide there until he may have town and castle; and his purpose then is to go into Pembrokeshire for he holds sure all the castles and towns in Kidwelly.

Gowersland and Glamorgan for the same countries have undertaken the siege of them until they be won.

'Excite the kings advisors that they should excite the king here
in all haste to avenge himself on some of his false traitors he has
cherished overmuch and to rescue the towns and castles in these
countries for I dread full sore there be few true to maintain them.'

Faireford wrote to the king:

'Ordain a remedy for the resistance and destruction of the
traitors which are daily reinforced and from time to time cause
great evil and destruction to your faithful subjects without any
resistance; considering my most gracious lord that if assistance
come not speedily, all the castles and towns and your loyal
subjects within them are in great peril and on the point of being
utterly ruined for default of succour and good government.'

The sheriffs of Herefordshire endorsed Faireford's view in
their letter to the king:

'. . . which force we have no power to resist without your
earnest aid and succour and this greatly displeases us, by reason of
the grievous costs and labours which it will be needful of us to
sustain.'

Richard Kingeston the Archdeacon of Hereford was even
more blunt in his despatch to the king:

'Letters are arriving from Wales containing intelligence by
which you may learn that the whole country is lost if you do not go
there as quickly as possible. For which reason may it please you to
prepare to set out with all the power that you can muster and
march day and night for the salvation of these parts. And may it
please you to reflect that it will be a great disgrace as well as a loss,
to lose or suffer to be lost in the beginning of your reign a country
which your noble ancestors have won and for so long a time
peaceably possessed. For people talk very unfavourably.'

On July 10 Hotspur was welcomed by the citizens of Chester and he immediately recruited them to his cause. The first move in the game had gone to him, and when the king heard the news on the 13th at Nottingham he ordered a forced march to Shrewsbury before that city, too, fell to the rebels. Happily for him the Welsh army which might have taken pro-Welsh Shrewsbury was trapped a hundred miles away at Laugharne Castle. Even had they been free to march to Hotspur's support they could scarcely have reached Shrewsbury before the king. And they were not free. They were trapped at Laugharne with the sea behind them and the Flemings in front. The tragic result was told in a letter from the jubilant burgesses of Caerleon to the burgesses of Monmouth of the final encounters on July 12.

'There was this day a battle between the worthy baron of Carewe and Owein Glyndour; and we do wish you to know that the night before the battle Owain was on purpose to have avoided him and to find out whether the way was clear to pass, if he had need of it. He sent 700 of his many to search the ways and there they met with the baron's men who slew everybody so there was none on that scene alive.'

The letter recounted a curious piece of gossip which shows that Owain was as much a servant of superstition as he was its master.

'He sent for Hopkyn ap Thomas of Gower to come and speak with him on truce and Hopkin came. Owain he prayed him, in as much as he held him a Master of Brut that he should tell him how and in what manner it should fall our for him; and he told him that he would be captured in a short time between Carmarthen and Gower and the taking would be under a black banner.

'Be glad and merry and dread you naught for you have no need.'

The burgesses' cheering news was the last of the letters of this little campaign which has survived. Owain escaped from the

Flemings' trap but by then it was too late, Shrewsbury had been fought and lost.

† † †

The adventure had begun well for Hotspur. In Chester, he took up quarters with Petronilla Clark the mother of one of his esquires and lost no time in exploiting the citizens' loyalty to Richard who, he claimed, would personally lead the fight against Henry. White Hart badges were passed from hand to hand when his army of 10,000 mustered at Sandiway a small village some ten miles from Chester. Its backbone was the company of Cheshire archers, ruthless men and even by 15th century standards an unsavoury crew. In Richard's reign they had been the weapon with which the king had forced repressive measures on his parliament. In his Merciless Parliament when more men were sentenced to death than at any one time in the whole of the Middle Ages in Britain, Cheshire archers had lined the walls of Westminster, the arrows in their drawn bows pointed at the hearts of the cowed parliamentarians.

A contemporary wrote of them:

'These men, being brutes by nature, were ready to execute any deed of wickedness and they soon waxed so wanton in their insolence that they regarded the king as their fellow and despised all others, even great lords. And these men were not of the gentry of ths shire but drawn from the plough, from the cobblers last and every other mechanic craft; so that those who at home were hardly thought worthy to take off their master's boots, thought themselves abroad, as good as a lord.'

Adam of Usk endorsed this view:

'Very evil; and in all places they oppressed Richard's subjects unpunished and beat and robbed them These men whither-soever the king went night and day, as if at war, kept watch in arms about him; everywhere committing adulteries, murders and other evils without end. And to such a pass did the king cherish them that he would not deign to listen to anyone who had complaint against them; nay rather he would disdain him as an enemy.'

To a rhymer of the period they were 'mystery men meddlers of wrongs who played with pole axes and the points of swords'.

This *corps d'élite* would support anyone who could pay them but not all the army which marched down through Whitchurch and Wem to Shrewsbury were ready to fight. The tenants of Lord Lestrange in the Hundred of Ellesmere were simple country people who joined the rebellion in the belief they were supporting Richard. The steward of their Lordship, Roger Kynaston, had summoned them to attend King Richard in Lestrange's name. At Myddle in Shropshire they discovered that Richard was not to lead them and demanded to be allowed to return home. It was too late. Under threats of hanging and beheading the villagers were marched on to die anyway at Shrewsbury.

On July 20 the king was in Stafford two days' march from Shrewsbury, thirty-two miles away. Hotspur had twenty-four hours' start on Henry but it was the king who won the race. With the speed of movement and decision which was his greatest military gift Henry doubled the marching pace of his army and by nightfall he had occupied Shrewsbury. When Hotspur's army halted under the town walls a few hours later it was Henry's leopards which menaced him from their banners above the gate, not the golden dragon of Glyndŵr which he must have been expecting to greet him.

It was a heavy blow, but the royal occupation of Shrewsbury and the non-appearance of the Welsh were not Hotspur's only disappointment. Hardyng, his librarian, who was on the campaign claimed Hotspur had letters from most of the great nobles in the country pledging their support yet few of them kept their word. Although his uncle, the Earl of Worcester, deserted the king for Hotspur, his father the Earl of Northumberland was struck by a diplomatic illness and did not arrive. The first of the 'loving complices' this appalling man was to desert, as he first fanned and then fled the flames of insurrection, was his own son. Hardyng's censure was bitter, but wholly deserved:

> His fayther came not out of Northumberland
> But failed him foul without wit or rede.

Only one course remained for Hotspur. It was to fall back on Chester and defend the city until the promised reinforcements arrived. But his men were weary after the two-day march from that city so he made camp three miles from Shrewsbury centre in the village of Berwick.

When they told him the name of the village he knew that his cause was lost. Like Glyndŵr, Hotspur had consulted a Master of Brut about the future and he had been told that he would die at Berwick. He had assumed that the town on the Tweed border had been meant and he had felt safe in the heart of the English countryside.

Such at any rate is the legend. Something certainly was troubling Hotspur that morning when he awoke in the manor house of William Bretton. Long after the battle the Bretton family treasured the long sword he left behind when he rode off at the head of his army. It was a strange aberration.

When Hotspur was dressed, his pages hung his dagger on his right side and threaded his stabbing sword through an iron ring from which it could be easily withdrawn, on his right. But he galloped off without the long sword which it was the final duty of his squire to hand him in the saddle.

Perhaps the news with which he had been awakened made him forgetful. Henry's 'Battle' force was advancing down the main Shrewsbury to Chester road while a light cavalry force commanded by the Prince of Wales was riding along the river bank to cut off the line of Hotspur's withdrawal to Chester. When he heard the news, Hotspur led his troops in flight across country to Harlescott the nearest point to Berwick on the Chester road and his only route to safety. His situation was unenviable. With trained soldiers a fighting retreat in good order was a workable manoeuvre, albeit a dangerous one, but Hotspur's was not a trained army. It contained good fighting soldiers, as they were to prove in the hours ahead, but its bulk was made up of peasants and the rabble of Chester, many of them duped to join in the belief that King Richard would lead. It was less than three days old as a fighting unit and there had not been time to test its temper. A successful retreat down thirty miles of road to Chester would have to be tightly controlled if it was not to degenerate into a panic-stricken flight. Hotspur's choice of Harlescott as a battle-field has been criticised. Yet there was no better place in the flat acres between Shrewsbury and Chester and his untried soldeirs needed the cohesion of battle if they were to remain an inte-grated fighting force.

Hotspur chose Harlescott because there was no choice.

Only one ridge running from east to west in the land round Harlescott gives advantage of ground. In an interesting echo of Humbleton Hotspur led his troops to the top and posted the Chester archers on a terrace below where they commanded the oncoming royal army along a 900 yard front. On the flat ground at the foot of the ridge, separating the two armies, were fields of growing peas, and in the hours before the battle Hotspur's pioneers were out amongst them, twining the tendrils of the plants into rudimentary trip wires to slow a cavalry attack.

The bloody discordance of fifteenth century warfare was orchestrated by a stately ritual. It began with the singing of Mass; and on Harlescott Ridge that day there was no shortage of celebrants. Hotspur's army including a large number of Cheshire clerics and, as the soldiers waited for the battle to begin, the bird-song of the July morning was drowned in plainsong from the ranks of both armies. Then Hotspur, bare-headed, his hair tight with sweat where his helmet had pressed it to his head, rode his horse at a walk until he stood, an isolated figure, between the cavalry and foot-soldiers and the line of Chester archers below him.

His speech that day was a simple one which Walsingham has preserved. The language was direct and evocative of the man. Deserted by the powerful nobles who had promised him their support, disapppointed in his hope of Welsh reinforcements and abandoned by his own father, this is what Hotspur told his soldiers on the ridge at Harlescott.

'We must desist from any further attempt at retreat and turn our arms on those who come against us. You see the royal banner, nor is there time to seek a passage through, even though we wished it.

'Stand, therefore, with steadfast hearts; for this day shall either promote us all if we conquer; or deliver us from a usurper, if we fall — and it is better to die in battle for the commonwealth than after battle by the sentence of the foe.'

It was now time to deliver a second message, more formal and as much for history as for the king who would receive it. Two of Hotspur's squires, Thomas Kynaston and Roger Salvayn, detached themselves from the line of mounted knights and carried Hotspur's challenge to the king. Hotspur loved military bands, he never went to war without one — and as his squires rode down, their horses picking a careful way through the twined tendrils of the pea crop, they were accompanied by the harsh music of drums and trumpet. Beyond the peas the squires spurred their destriers into a canter to ride the five hundred yards across the fields which separated the two armies. Now it was the king's music which played its accompaniment to their ride, their hair streaming from their bare heads. They needed no helmets, a herald's office was sacred during the prelude to battle and they were greeted, traditionally, with gifts when they delivered their challenge. In the defiance which Kynaston and Salvayn made before the king at Shrewsbury many of the inconsistencies of Hotspur's earlier conduct are resolved. Hotspur's declaration can be seen as a justification for motives less glorious than he claimed. Yet his refusal of a knighthood from the king's hands at his coronation and his lack-lustre performance in Wales, set against his brilliant defence of his own lands, argue that he was never in sympathy with the king's usurpation.

In the name of his appalling father, his uncle Thomas Percy, Earl of Worcester, Hotspur told the king that he intended:

'. . . to prove with our hands, personally, on this day, against you Henry, Duke of Lancaster, your accomplices and supporters, that you have unjustly assumed and named yourself King of England without just title, but by thy treachery and the violence of thy supporters; because, when you entered England after your exile you swore to us at Doncaster, upon the Holy Gospels, held and likewise kissed by you personally, that you would not lay claim to the kingdom, or to the royal estate, but only to your own heritage and the heritage of your wife in England. And that Richard, at that time our Lord and King should reign to the end of his life, guided by the good counsel of the Lords Spiritual and Temporal. You imprisoned that same Lord, thy King and ours, beneath the Tower of London, until through fear of death he resigned the kingdoms of England and France and renounced all his right in the aforesaid kingdoms, and his other dominions and lands across the sea.

'Upon the plea of which resignation and renunciation by the advice of your supporters, and by the public clamour of the vulgar populace, collected together at Westminster by you and your accomplices, you crowned yourself king of the aforesaid kingdoms, contrary to your oath — and therefore you are perjured and false.'

After accusing Henry of levying taxes against his own sworn word the denunciation continued:

'Likewise we aver, say and intend to prove that although you swore to us upon the same Holy Gospels, at the same time and place, that Richard, our Lord and King and yours to be imprisoned in your Castle of Pontefract without his consent or the decrees of the Lords of the Kingdom, and to suffer hunger, cold thirst and cold for fifteen days and as many nights and to perish by murder, which is horrible to be heard amongst Christians; wherefore you are perjured and false.

'Likewise we aver, say, and intend to prove that as soon as Richard our Lord and King and yours, was so horribly murdered as above stated, you seized, usurped and took forcible possession of the Kingdom of England and the name and honour of King of France, unjustly and contrary to your oath, from Edmund Mortimer, Earl of March, then the nearest and direct heir of England and France, immediately and hereditarily to succeed after the decease of the said Richard; wherefore you are perjured and false.'

Henry was accused of rigging parliament with men of his own faction and finally Hotspur came to the personal cause of his quarrel with the king.

'Likewise we aver, say and intend to prove that when Edmund Mortimer, brother of Roger Mortimer, late Earl of March and Ulster, was captured by Owen Glendower in open war in thy cause, and still kept in prison and iron chains, you proclaimed he was captured by strategem and would not allow any treaty for his liberation, neither through himself nor us, his relations and friends, wherefore we treated for his liberation with the said Owen, with our own property, on which account you have regarded us as traitors, and likewise have craftily and secretly compassed and imagined the death and final destruction of our persons.'

Custom demanded that before a battle the king should confer knighthoods on aspirants in the royal army. On the day before, in Shrewsbury, the esquires had been ritually bathed to cleanse them from sin. After the bath they had been dressed in a white linen robe, to remind them that their flesh must be free from stain. Over the white robe a crimson one was hung, in token that they would shed their blood in the cause of Christ. The aspirants wore brown silk trunk hose to remind them of death and the earth in which they would lie and a white girdle was tied round their loins as a warning against promiscuity.

The squires had spent the night watching over their arms in Shrewsbury Abbey. Now they received knighthoods at the hands of a man who had just been accused of the murder of a king. They lined up before Henry on the battlefield with their swords, which they had not yet earned the right to wear at their side, hanging from their necks. They handed them in turn to the king who struck each esquire on the right shoulder with the flat side of the weapon and kissed them in brotherly adoption.

It was all part of the game of war, and the older knights who had already received the honour were approving spectators. Death was a hazard for them but it was not a certainty, the law of ransom would protect their lives. But there were thousands on both sides for whom it was no game. For the common soldier with hand-me-down breast-plates, dented and scratched; for the archers who would bear the brunt of the attack and for the host of pioneers and foot soldiers without any protection at all the long ceremony must have been agony. They waited in their files while the king conferred on his nephew, the Earl of Stafford, the office of Constable of England recently held by the Earl of Northumberland.

Despite his numerical superiority the king was uneasy about the battle and he made a final effort to prevent the encounter. Thomas Prestbury, the Abbot of Shrewsbury, was despatched to Hotspur's lines with an offer of peace, pardon and the redress of grievance. Hotspur obviously shared the king's unease. In his turn he sent the Earl of Worcester to make a more private statement of his grievance to the king. His choice of emissary was unwise. He could hardly have done worse if he had sent Douglas, itching now for the battle to begin. The Earl's first words to the king were a calculated insult, he told him:

'You rob the country every year and always say you have nothing, you make no payments, keep no house and you are not the rightful heir.'

The king replied that he had been chosen by the country and that the taxes he levied were needed for the government of the realm. It was a reasonable answer and he followed it with a final offer of friendship. He urged the Earl: 'Put yourself in my hand and trust in my favour'.

It was useless.

'I trust not in your grace,' Worcester replied.

'I pray God that thou mayest have to answer for the blood to be shed here this day and not I,' the king told him in dismissal. As Worcester galloped back to his own lines the king ordered his battle formations on the field still known as the King's Croft. The main body was under his own command with the Earl of Stafford; the second battalion was commanded by the Prince of Wales.

The waiting was not quite over and for one man, at least, it proved too much. In the last minutes before the battle there was a sudden disturbance in Hotspur's ranks and a horse came galloping down the hill. Followed by the jeers of his companions, Richard Horkesley galloped across the quiet meadows which were soon to be the field of battle and was swallowed up in the royal ranks. A spy, perhaps, returning to the king at the last moment? Nothing else is known.

Nothing could delay the battle now. With a glance at the Prince of Wales on his left the king at last gave the order to advance.

'Trumpets sound.'

'Banners forward.'

The waiting was over.

On Humbleton Hill the English long bow had demonstrated its superiority over the shorter Scottish bow and re-stated its mastery over cavalry. At Shrewsbury long-bow met long-bow for the first time. The result was carnage. Henry's bowmen were the first to engage the enemy. Running almost double, their bows half drawn, they crossed the meadow between the armies to shorten the range of their arrows. But it was the more seasoned Chester archers, motionless on their crest, who had the advantage. The moment Henry's archers reached the half-way point between the two armies, before they could sight their own bows, arrows rained down on them. The first ranks died where they stood. The survivors scrambled over the fallen and ran through the hail of arrows and some even reached the foot of the ridge, but it was useless. No-one could withstand the Chester bowmen and at length the royal archers broke and ran back for the safety of the advancing column of cavalry. In their confusion they smashed into the first rank of the king's men-at-arms, panicking their horses. It might have been the deciding moment of the battle. As the horses plunged and reared, unhorsing their riders, the king's battalion was at the mercy of the finest bowmen in Europe. Within range now of the armour-piercing arrows they could be picked off almost at leisure by the bowmen on the ridge. The tactics which had won the day at Humbleton would have been just as successful at Shrewsbury. The scenario was identical. The enemy archers were in flight, the cavalry a confused and demoralised mass of rearing horses and cursing knights. The situation was made for the devastating fire-power of the Chester archers from their commanding position on the ridge. But if the scenario was familiar there had been a change in casting. At Shrewsbury the Earl of Douglas was Hotspur's ally, the Earl of March was advising the king. Douglas's advice to Hotspur was to cost him the battle.

Romantic historians have made much of the gallant charge Hotspur made with the 'Tine Man' at the head of a troop of thirty horsemen into the thick of the royal army. Down the hill they rode and through the peas, armour glinting, pennants blown flat against their lance tips. The shock of their impact sent the king's bodyguard reeling. The royal standard crashed to the ground. Stafford and Sir Walter Blount were killed and in the slaughter which followed Douglas struck down three knights in royal armour. The slaying of three counterfeit kings was an oddly typical act as the whole mad charge had been. A wiser general would have been content to wait on the ridge until the archers had thoroughly demoralised the royal army.

Henry himself was at the heart of the fight. It was reported later that he personally slew thirty-six men-at-arms but his own losses were heavy. One after the other his best leaders fell. The

Prince of Wales was badly wounded in the eye. The dead included
Sir Hugh Stanley, Sir John Clifton, Sir John Kokaine, Sir Nicholas
Gamsell, Sir John Calveley, Sir Hugh Mortimer and Sir Gonsill
(sic). Sir John Massy died at the king's feet wiping out at last the
stain of Conway. At first the fierce fighting seemed to be routing
the royal force. Screaming 'Esperaunce Percy' and more
revealingly 'Percy for King' Hotspur's remaining troops
abandoned their tactical superiority on the ridge and galloped
down to join in the scrum. So far the battle had been between
Hotspur and the king's force but though the Prince of Wales
himself had been wounded by an arrow his own troops had not
yet been involved. It was now time for him to intervene. As the
king fell back the Prince brought his troops in a wide arc and
smashed into the rear of Hotspur's army. The rebel force was in a
trap and the fighting which followed was the most bitter and
bloody in any English civil war. When it was over Hotspur and
two thousand and ninety-one of his followers were dead, among
them two hundred Cheshire knights and esquires. There are no
figures for casualties on the royal side but they too must have
been severe.

The news of Hotspur's death ended the battle. It was shouted
by the king and his knights and the rebels broke and ran. Douglas
in fleeing managed somehow in that flat countryside, 'tining' to
the last, to fall from a crag and break his leg, but in the end he
came off best. In admiration of his valour Henry set him free
without ransom and he was able to hobble off to losses new.
Worcester, the Baron of Kinderton and Sir Richard Vernon were
less fortunate. Two days later, after a drum-head trial in Shrewsbury, all three were executed.

After the battle, Hotspur's body was brought to the king. In the
first moments of victory, Henry was disposed to behave chival-
rously towards his enemy. The king's nephew Thomas Neville,
Lord Furnival, was also a kinsman of Hotspur. The body was
handed over to him and the king decreed that it should be buried
with all the honours due to Hotspur's rank. Impulsive gestures
are soon regretted. The king had already suffered from the resur-
rection of dead heroes for political ends. The day after the burial

he ordered the exhumation of Hotspur's body. For several days, jammed between two millstones at the pillory in Shrewsbury market place, the decomposing remains were exhibited to the commons, guarded by two soldiers. Finally the putrefying corpse was publicly beheaded and quartered and the quarters sent to the four principal cities in England. The heads of the Baron of Kinderton and Richard Vernon were buried with their bodies but Worcester's head joined the grim trophy display on London Bridge.

Battlefield church which now stands over the great pit 126 feet wide and 65 feet long in which the dead of both sides are buried is the only church in Britain built as a war memorial. On Christmas Eve that year, Henry ordered the establishment of the church and a college where masses were to be sung in perpetuity for the souls of the dead soldiers. But the king had little time to celebrate his victory. In Wales the rebels were increasing their attacks on the remaining royal strongholds. A letter from William Beauchamp written during the autumn which followed the battle of Shrewsbury illumines a small corner of the campaign.

'May it please your royal excellency to know that I gave leave and licence to your royal liege, John de Assheby, a soldier of mine, who has done me good and loyal service at Abergavenny, to go from that place of Abergavenny as far as to Hereford, to have an interview there with his wife, returning to Abergavenny that day after the next following, but he arrived at that time of his evil fortune (*illegible in manuscript*) . . . the rebels and robbers of Wales met him and his guide and took him in spite of the same guide, between whom he was on the point of being put to death, in like manner as two others of my soldiers were taken and slain, had it not been that by the especial grace of God and his own good fortune one of the said rebels offered and proferred for him ten marks to save his life, to the intent that he should obtain the release of his brother who was held in your royal town of Brecon.'

This sad tale of families caught up in war is followed by the familiar plea:

'. . . I would most humbly beseech you, and in great bitterness of heart, that it would please you of your good grace and great compassion to remember my poor and suffering person who am in exceeding great trouble and distress at present and to extend to me with all your speed your succour and gracious aid in this case; which is very perilous and pitiable; otherwise I hold myself destroyed this present day.'

Every messenger brought similar pleas. On September 3 Richard Kingeston, the Dean of Windsor, wrote:

'. . . there are come into our country more than four hundred of the rebels of Owen, Glyn, Talgard and many other rebels besides, from the Marches of Wales, and they have captured and robbed within your county of Hereford many men and beasts in great numbers, our truce notwithstanding.

'. . . for the preservation of your said county and all the March to send me this night or to-morrow early morning at the latest my most honoured Master Beaufort or some person who is willing and able to labour with one hundred lances and six hundred archers, until your most gracious arrival to the salvation of all; for otherwise my most dread Lord I hold all your country to be destroyed. For all the hearts of your faithful lieges in our country, with the commons, are utterly lost; and for this, that they hear you are not coming to this place in your own person (which God Avert). You will find for certain that, if you do not come in your own person to await your rebels in Wales, you will not find a single gentleman that will stop in your said country. Wherefore, for God's sake, think on your best friend, God, and thank him as he hath deserved of you; and leave nought that you do not come for no man that may counsel you the contrary; for, by the truth that I shall be to you yet, this day the Welshmen suppose and trust that you shall not come there, and therefore, for God's love, make them false men. And it please you of your high Lordship to have me excused of my coming to you, for in good faith I have naught here left with me over two men for to withstand the malice of the rebels this day.'

Carreg Cennen, as it might have appeared before it was dismantled in 1462.
(Crown Copyright.)

Mediaeval Seige Warfare. (By permission of the British Library.)

Dignified and reasoned though this letter was its message was unmistakable. The contest was now between Henry IV and Owain Glyndŵr. Only the king could save his Welsh kingdom. Henry could not ignore so direct an appraisal. In mid-September he once again left Hereford at the head of an army. Superficially it was successful. The royal columns marched through Brecon and down the Valley of the Usk, receiving homage everywhere and setting up new chains of command in areas where Owain had been dominant. But no sooner had the king crossed back into England than Henry Don rose with a mixed force of Welsh and Bretons and laid siege to Kidwelly Castle. It was as though the king had never marched.

In North Wales the rebel army achieved complete ascendancy over the forces of the Crown. Welsh raiding parties forded the Dee at will to raid the English communities on the far bank, despite water-borne patrols by the garrisons from Rhuddlan, Prestatyn and Coleshill. So strong were the rebels now that outside Chester defensive ditches were dug and timber barricades built across the rebels' line of advance. In the city the authorities panicked. Welshmen were forbidden to live within the walls and any found there after dusk were summarily beheaded. They were barred from taverns and all strangers were searched at the city gates for arms. Visitors were allowed only 'a little knife to cut their meat with'. On August 25 the Prince of Wales called on Sir William de Stanley, Sir William de Poole, John Litherland and John of Moels, the Conservators and Guardians of the Hundreds of the Wirral, to 'appoint watches and make ditches, hedges and other impediments on the sea coast of the County of Flint against the coming of Glyndŵr now in the Marches of the County of Chester'. Yet at the height of the emergency Chester traders still sold arms and ale at Malpas market to rebels who swam them across the Dee into Wales.

Harlech Castle was once again besieged by the Welsh, but there was no hope of a relief column now. Robin Holland of Eglwys Fach who commanded the rebels at Harlech had already achieved one notable success in the capture of the Constable of the Castle, John Hennore. He had fallen into Holland's hands when he led a

raiding party from the castle. The garrison soon became un-
comfortably aware that his successor, William Hunt, wanted to
join his predecessor in captivity as speedily as possible. Only his
arrest by his own soldiers prevented him from handing over this
vital stronghold to the Welsh. He was locked in the castle
dungeon and two of his officers 'Sir Vivian' and Favian Collier, a
local man, took over the command. They fought valiantly but
sickness diminished the garrison until only five English soldiers
and sixteen Welshmen remained. Hunt and two yeomen, Jack
Mercer and Harry Baker, escaped at the first opportunity and
gave themselves up to the rebels.

Harlech was not the only castle in danger. From Chester
William Venables, the Deputy Warden of the Marches whose
brother, Richard, had been beheaded by the king after
Shrewsbury wrote to Henry:

'Robert Parys the Deputy Constable of Caernarvon has
apprised us through a woman, because there was no man who
dared come, for neither man nor woman dare carry letters on
account of the rebels of Wales, that Owain Glyndŵr with the
French and all his other power is preparing to assault the town
and castle of Caernarvon and to begin this enterprise with
engines, sowes (hide-covered huts beneath which miners could
burrow at castle walls) and ladders of great length; and in the
town there are not more than twenty-eight fighting men, which
is all too small a force; for eleven of the more able men who were
there at the last siege of the place are dead; some of the wounds
they received at the time of the assault and others of the plague;
so the said castle and town are in imminent danger.'

Some Constables preferred to adopt more warlike postures in
their despatches to the king. Henry of Scarisbrooke wrote from
Conway:

'I durst lay my head that 200 men in Conway and 200 in
Caernarvon would be sufficient to protect the two counties with

ease and the inhabitants, with the exception of four or five gentlemen and a few vagabonds would gladly pay dues to the English for protection rather than suffer from the rebels.'

Privately Scarisbrooke was less sanguine. In a more realistic letter to Venables he wrote:

'Owain has been to Harlech Castle and is in accord with all the men that are there, save only seven, for to have deliverance of the castle at a certain daye for a certain sum of gold. If it be right ordained it is lost and so is all the country thereabout.'

French involvement in the siege of Caernarvon was no new development. Earlier that autumn French privateers had made a series of attacks on the English coast. Bretons aided Don in his siege of Kidwelly and on Anglesey a force of 200 French ambushed the train of Meredith ap Cynwrig, a tax collector, as he rode to Beaumaris Castle.

On the south coast of England French raids were so numerous that a defence alliance was signed between coastal towns. Only Plymouth stood apart, a decision its townspeople were to regret. When a combined French and Breton fleet were sighted off the town the fighting men from other towns nearby rushed to its aid, but the Plymouth shopkeepers rewarded them by doubling the price of their goods. In the hot words which followed the Plymouth men haughtily declined outside help. Twelve hours after the last would-be rescuers had left the French landed and plundered the town 'without hindrance' until three o'clock on the afternoon following. When they left they burned the town to the ground and a chastened Plymouth at once sent ships to join Dartmouth and Bristol in a reprisal raid under the command of William of Wilford. It was very successful. Off Brest William took six French ships and on the night of his arrival off Brittany four more with cargoes of iron, oil and tallow. At Belle Isle thirty-four more vessels were taken and 1,000 casks of wine looted from Rochelle. At the head of 4,000 men Wilford penetrated six leagues into Brittany burning villages and laying waste, collecting forty more ships on his way. When the Captain of Brittany, the Sieur de Calais, sent a sergeant of arms to complain William told him shortly that he wished to burn half Brittany 'for his satisfaction'. It was not the sort of activity calculated to win Henry IV any friends in France.

VII

BETTER TO DIE IN A BATTLE

I N 1404 HENRY IV conceded defeat. When parliament met in January, the king, worn out by endless civil war, and suffering the result of a succession of nervous crises which was to end in his death, transferred overall command of the Welsh War (for it was a rebellion no longer) to his son, Prince Henry. Edmund, the self-indulgent Duke of York, had been forced, before his death in 1403, to put one side his ambitious plans to build an abbey round the Parish Church on his estate at Fotheringay and to assume command in South Wales. York had been used to higher office. During the minority of Richard II who was his nephew he had been Regent of England, but he had gone anyway. Now the Earl of Arundel, son of Owain's early patron, became Royal Lieutenant in North Wales.

For Prince Henry it was an empty command. The real Prince of Wales now was Owain Glyndŵr and by the end of the year only three castles remained firmly in English hands. The land belonged again to the Welsh. Caerleon, Caerphilly, Newport and Usk had all fallen and the garrisons of the other castles were in a pitiful state. When Cardiff Castle was forced to surrender, the supplies of 24 men-at-arms and 479 archers were reduced to 4lb of powder, twenty-eight stone cannon balls and forty 'gads' for their guns. Food had dwindled to three barrels of salt meat, a pipe of salmon, beans and a little beer. Radnor, which Sir John Greindor surrendered in 1405, had been defended by only nine men-at-arms and 22 archers. The castle of Cefnllys on the Ithon was burned, and the rich estates of Knighton and Cnwclas; even the king's own lands round Ogmore, were laid waste.

In North Wales the English were even worse hit. There were only eight men-at-arms and 108 archers to defend Flint, Rhuddlan, Conway, Beaumaris and Caernarvon. Henry was at his lowest ebb. Not only was the royal treasury empty, the king was deeply in debt and the soldiers in the North were owed a full year's pay.

Owain's star, in contrast, was in the ascendant. He commanded a fighting force of 30,000 men and his kingdom was financially secure. After Hotspur's death he polarised the opposition to the crown all over the British Isles. Religious communities in England were among his supporters. At a time when Henry's credit had been exhausted and further loans were given only grudgingly by the magnates, huge drafts of money were being smuggled by monks out of England to Owain.

In the years before Shrewsbury the rebellion had lacked firm purpose. Its drive was dissipated in a series of raids which, though successful, did nothing to create the principality to which Owain now aspired. After Shrewsbury Owain the statesman began to emerge. Now he was able to negotiate from a position of strength for an alliance with France, the hereditary enemy of England. The support of the Percys, though temporarily in eclipse still powerful figures, made his cause attractive to ambitious men who had attached themselves to Henry at the time of his rise to power. These men were administrators, skilled in diplomacy, who could create the frame on which the emerging Welsh kingdom would be re-built. With their guidance and advice Owain began to exploit his new power. An embryonic civil service began to show itself. In the years to come, proposals for a self-governing Welsh church and the creation of two universities to train the new kingdom's bureaucrats were set out.

Much of the credit for bringing Glyndŵr to political maturity had gone to Gruffydd Young, the man who became his Chancellor. Save that he was illegitimate nothing is known of his early life. With a bastard's tenacity and a natural talent for the politics of power, he had become a force in the church. By 1390, when by a papal mandate, he was granted the living of Llanbadarn Fawr, he already held a canonry and prebend at Bangor, the church of Llanynys in Dyffryn Clwyd and a contested canonry and prebend at Abergele. He was a bachelor of law and a doctor of decrees. In the early years of Henry's reign he had been a valued administrator at court. In 1407, after a change of loyalties, he had become so powerful in Owain Glyndŵr's court that he was able to survive the purges of recurring papal schisms; even ousting his own superior and another of Owain's councillors, Lewis Byfort, from the Bishopric of Bangor. Owain had the men and in 1404, he found the setting for his new court.

Harlech Castle stands on a cliff over-looking a wide plain. Today there are factories at its foot, a railway station and a housing estate. In the fifteenth century it was at the sea's edge and impossible to conquer by feat-of-arms, except by prolonged and expensive siege warfare. In 1404 it had a new commander, Sir John Burton, and a garrison, recently increased, of twelve men-at-arms and 45 archers. Even today, in partial ruin, Harlech is a magnificent castle and a superbly menacing piece of military engineering. An embattled wall with loopholes runs the length of the outer ward from the north east corner to the Watergate and the armoured dock which was then at the sea's edge. It had cost Edward I the modern equivalent of a million pounds and taken two years to build. The eastern front of the castle which faces inland had walls between nine-and-a-half and twelve feet thick. From its towers a handful of archers could maintain a withering cross-fire along the entire length of its walls. A moat running round two sides of the castle from cliff edge to cliff edge gave further protection from assault.

Its importance to Glyndŵr far transcended its strategic value. The castle is built on one of the most important sites in Wales. On its rock, according to the Red Book of Hengest from which some of the legends of the *Mabinogi* were taken, was the palace of Bendigeidfran, the pre-Celtic king of all Britain. He lived there with his sister, Branwen of the White Neck 'the fairest damsel in the world'. In the 14th century, after his defeat, the palace of the last native Welsh prince, Llewellyn, was moved from its site four miles away at Ystumgwern and re-erected against a wall of the inner ward at Harlech.

It finally fell to Owain by bribery, as the English had prophesied, and not by feat of arms. Exactly how is not known, but it became the symbol of the new Welsh kingdom; and the court which Owain assembled there was a brilliant one. His fighting generals, Rhys Gethin, the victor of Pilleth, the Anglesey Tudors, Robert ap Jevan of Ystymcegid and Rhys Ddu, planned their campaigns there. Picturesque guerilla leaders like Cadogan of the Battle Axe, who led the tribes of the Rhondda, drank in Llewellyn's Hall. Cadogan was a special favourite of Owain who summoned him with the message 'Cadogan whet thy axe'. When he received this order, Cadogan set off round his glens sharpening the axe's edge and the sound of the whestsone against the iron was enough to bring both tribesmen and women running to his side. The administrators, no doubt, formed a quieter group. They were led by Byfort and Young and Owain's brother-in-law John Hanmer, whose brother Philip had fought with Owain from the first raid in Ruthin. John, a shrewder, calculating man had held his hand, even inheriting his outlawed brother's estates, until he was sure that Owain was winning. Then he joined, too.

Glyndŵr's quarters in the gatehouse had been the residence of the Castle Constable. The rooms were lofty and lighted, in the walls that overlooked the inner court, by traceried windows. Those which over-looked the town were smaller, barred and defensible. There was a private chapel and an impressive staircase from the main door to the inner court below. His new son-in-law, Mortimer, his daughter and their children took up residence in the tower which bears their name.

Iolo Goch, an old man now, was a frequent visitor, delighted at the success of his patron.

> Here's the life I've sighed for long
> Abashed is now the Saxon throng
> And Britons have a British Lord
> Whose emblem is the conquering sword
> There's none I trow but knows him well

The hero of the watery dell
Owain of bloody spear in field
Owain his country's strongest shield
A sovereign bright in grandeur drest
Whose frown afrights the bravest breast.

In keeping with his new dignity, Owain now assumed the
trappings of royalty. He took a more impressive coat of arms to
replace the dragon *rampant* under which he had fought as a rebel.
On the bronze bosses of his horses' martingales were the four
lions *rampant,* counterchanged in gold and red, the ancient Royal
arms of Gwynedd. His state seal which he fixed to all his
documents shows Glyndŵr as an armed warrior on one side and a
sceptred prince, seated, on the obverse. The news of the new
court spread all over Europe and he began to receive envoys from
England's many enemies on the continent. In Rome, taking a rest
from his constant petitions to Henry to allow him to return,
Adam of Usk enviously noted Owain's new power:

'Owain and his hill men, even in their mysery, usurping the
right of conquest and other marks of royalty, albeit to his own
confusion, held, or counterfeited or made pretences of holding
parliaments.'

There was no pretence. In a characteristic lawyer's search for
precedent Glyndŵr had modelled his parliaments on firm
foundations. In the 10th century King Hywel Dda had temporarily united the warring tribes of Wales under his rule. He had
codified and improved Welsh law and set up the rudiments of a
national parliament. Owain took up this concept, summoning
four representatives from each commote in his kingdom to
Machynlleth and Harlech where he marked the formal beginning
of his reign with a splendid coronation attended by envoys from
many European courts. His ascendancy to the throne of Wales
was not to be untroubled by incident and he was to suffer at least
one assassination attempt.
David ap Llewelyn ap Howel, Davy Gam or 'Squint eyed Davy'
was a Brecon land-owner and a kinsman of Owain. He was an

unprepossessing dwarf with long, simian arms and a blazing mop of red hair who, in his youth, had been forced to fly to England after murdering a neighbour, Long Richard, in the main street of Brecon. He had been taken in by John of Gaunt and brought up with the man who was now Henry IV. He was wholly devoted to the Bolingbrokes and conceived the notion of stabbing Owain as he walked to his first parliament. It was a typically brave gesture, for even had he been successful he would have certainly been killed by Owain's supporters. In the event, the plot was discovered; he was arrested and brought before Owain, who ordered him to be put to death. Fortunately for 'Davy Gam' relatives interceded and the sentence was commuted to imprisonment, which ended with the defeat of Owain. Davy died on the field of Agincourt with his son-in-law Roger Vychan. He is reckoned by some to be the original of Shakespeare's Fluellen.

Owain was not a forgiving man. On a raid in Brecon, he burned down Davy's manor at Cyrnigwern on the banks of the River Honddu. As he rode away, Owain saw one of Davy's squires and improvised a bitter little poem.

> Shouldst thou a little red man descry
> Asking about his dwelling fair
> Tell him it under a bank doth lie
> And its brow the mark of the coal doth bear.

Owain was swift to punish treachery. A cousin, Hywel Sele, was a king's man. In an effort to bring them together, the Abbot of Cymer in mid-Wales had arranged a meeting between the two men at Sele's manor of Nannau in the mountains near Dolgellau. Sele was a noted archer and, apparently reconciled, the two men went out hunting. Owain pointed out a stag, a difficult shot, and invited Sele to bring it down. Instead, at the moment of aim, Sele turned and loosed his arrow at Owain. The arrow was deflected by the armour Owain wore beneath his coat and within seconds Sele was dead. Owain's followers burned down Sele's manor. His body lay undiscovered for several years, until a skeleton was found crammed in the hollow trunk of an oak tree. A cousin, Gryffyth ap

Gwn of Ardudwy, alarmed by the fire from Sele's mansion,
arrived with a party of men to remonstrate with Owain. He and
all his followers were slaughteı d for their pains, and Gryffyth's
two manors of Berthlwyd and Cefn Coch were also razed.

Effective though these measures were in the family circle,
more sophisticated forms of persuasion were necessary if Owain
was to win the support of the European courts. Of these, the court
of the mentally disturbed Charles VI in Paris was clearly the most
sympathetic to England's enemies. The charitable ascribed the
derangement of Charles to a fright he received at the sudden
appearance of a hermit, which caused his horse to bolt whilst
hunting. The less charitably inclined put his malady down to the
recurring appearances of his brother, the Duke of Orleans, in the
bed of his Queen, Isabelle, a lady of considerable appetites.
Whatever the cause, England's behaviour over the past sixty
years and her insistence on sovereign rights on the French
mainland had done little to restore the King's balance. Richard II
had sought to end the differences by his marriage to Charles's
seven year old daughter Isabelle, but the usurpation had ended
any hopes from the alliance. In 1402, escorted by Thomas Percy
the Constable of England and a train of knights, the child queen
was brought to Leulingham between Bolougne and Calais. She
was handed over with exquisite courtesy to Waleran, the Count of
St Pol, the Bishop of Chartres and the Lord de Heugeville. St Pol
in his turn escorted Isabelle to a nearby hill where the Dukes of
Burgundy and Bourbon were waiting to take her to Paris. Only
one significant omission was made. Isabelle's rich dowry was not
amongst the possessions she brought back to France.
Charles was furious. He could not bear to name Henry as king.
At their kindest his documents refer to 'our cousin of England' or
'Henry of Lancaster'. More often it was 'Our Adversary of
England' or the 'Successor to the late king of England'.
In happier times Henry had ratified Richard's peace treaty and
himself signed a separate treaty of friendship with Louis, the
Duke of Orleans, but the affair of Isabelle's dowry put an end to
all agreements. Orleans was so angry that he issued a personal

challenge to the English king. It was the beginning of a curious correspondence.

Orleans wrote:

'Considering idleness as the bane of lords of high birth who do not employ themselves in arms, and thinking I can no way better seek renown than by proposing to you to meet me at an appointed place, each of us accompanied with one hundred knights and esquires without reproach, there to combat together until one of the parties shall surrender. We will not employ any incantations that are forbidden by Holy Church (The Duke had lately been touched by a scandal involving witchcraft) but make use of the bodily strength granted us by God, having armour as may be the most agreeable of his person and with the usual arms; that is to say, lance, battle axe, sword and dagger and each to employ there as he shall think most to his advantage, without aiding himself of any bodkins, hooks, bearded darts, poisoned needles or razors . . .'

Henry waited six months before he replied and then it was with a letter clearly designed to infuriate the status-conscious Duke. He wrote with icy disdain:

'. . . We are not bound to answer any such demands unless made by persons of equal rank with ourselves.'

The letter went on:

'. . . Whenever we may think it convenient we shall visit our possessions on your side of the sea, accompanied by such number of persons as we may please; at which time if you shall think proper you may assemble as many persons as you may judge expedient to acquire honour in the accomplishment of your courageous desires — and should it please God and my Lord St George you shall not depart until your request be so fully complied with that you shall find yourself satisfied by a combat between us two personally so long as it may please God to suffer it, which mode I should prefer to prevent any greater shedding of Christian blood.'

The letter ended with the snub supreme.

'Should you wish that those of your party be without reproach, be more cautious in future of your letters, your promises and your seal.'

The calculated affront struck home. In his reply Orleans abandoned the knightly forms for the insult direct and incidentally exposed the motive behind his first 'disinterested' challenge.

'. . . in regard to your ignorance, or pretended ignorance, whether my letter could have been addressed to you; your name was on it, such as you were always called by your parents when they were alive. I had not indeed given you your new titles at length because I do not approve of the way you have attained them . . .

'. . . How could you suffer my much redoubted lady the Queen of England to return so desolate to this country after the death of her lord, despoiled, by your rigour and cruelties, of her dower, which you detain from her?

'As I am so nearly related to her I will cheerfully meet you in single combat or with any number you please . . .'

Orleans was never to get his wish. In the last letter of this correspondence Henry impishly tweaked the barb he had been inserting with such joy.

'. . . it seems by your present letter that this desire for combat has taken a frivolous turn and that you wish for a war of words . . .'

Little wonder that when Owain's emissaries arrived from Wales their reception at the French Court was rapturous.

Owain chose Young and John Hanmer to handle the negotiations between 'Owain by the Grace of God Prince of Wales' and 'Our Cousin the King of France'. When they left Dolgellau on May 10 the two men carried with them the letter in which Owain oulined his proposals for an alliance.

'To all who will examine these letters, greeting. Know ye that on account of the affection and sincere regard which the illustrious prince, the Lord Charles, by the same grace, King of the French, has up to the present time borne towards us and our subjects and of his grace bearing daily, we desire to cleave to him and to his subjects as by merit we are held to this purpose. Wherefore we make, ordain and constitute by these presents Master Griffith Yonge, Doctor of Canon Law, Chancellor and John de Hanmer, our well beloved kinsman our true and legal ambassadors proctors, factors, negotiators and special nuncios, giving and conceding to our same ambassadors, and to both of them by himself and in full, general power and special command in such manner that there shall not be a better condition of negotiation, but that which one of them shall commence the other of them has power to follow, consider and complete for us, and in our name concerning and over a perpetual league with the aforesaid most illustrious prince and of conducting, making and confirming the same league on our part, and of undertaking whatsoever suitable oath necessary in that part, and of the making of letters obligatory of this kind concerning the league, and of giving or granting for us whatsoever suitable oath necessary in that part in our stead, and of the making of letters obligatory of this kind, concerning the league and of giving and granting for us whatsoever other security may incidentally be necessary on their part, or of seeking and receiving the giving of similar security necessary in the material premises from the aforesaid most illustrious prince, the Lord Charles, By the Grace of God, King of France . . .'

The journey from Wales to France in the single masted sailing ships of the time could take as long as ten days in bad weather yet there were no doubt many in Harlech who envied the two ambassadors — for the French court was the most dazzling in Europe. Its grand balls and masques were internationally famous and its banquets were staggering, often literally so. The first book of *haute cuisine* cookery ever compiled was written by Charles's 'First Squire of the Kitchen', Guillaume Tirel, who had served his father, Charles V. Also from his father Charles had inherited a fork, a rarity outside Italy, which that monarch has used to eat his favourite dish, toasted cheese sprinkled with sugar and powdered cinnamon. It was a time of culinary invention. It was Queen Isabelle who devised the written menu to describe the dishes Tirel created.

In private the king dined simply, on capons in cinnamon sauce, chickens cooked in herbs and spices, cabbages — a rare concession to the vegetable garden which was little used except for medicines — and venison. State Banquets such as those given in honour of Young and Hanmer were more lavish affairs. Heavily spiced dishes were accompanied by champagne, the staple drink of the royal family, clarets from Bordeaux, drunk regrettably young, Beaune, and Chablis. Sadly the manners of the diners did not always match the quality of the fare. 'Courtesy Books', the mediæval manuals of etiquette, abounded in the fifteenth century. The advice the authors thought it necessary to give their readers is alarming. At a time when even the greatest of nobles scooped food in his hands from a communal dish, admonitions not to scratch crotches, pick noses and to keep fingers clean would seem unnecessary in polite society. Not so. The books advised that when an itch became unbearable the diners should use a portion of their dress to scratch themselves. Gnawed bones, the books warned, should be thrown on the floor where they could decompose slowly in the rushes — which were only replaced annually — and not put back in the serving dish. Oddly, in this careless society, drunkenness was frowned upon. It was considered impolite to drink more than three times from the wine cup which circulated the table during dinner.

The negotiations for the Franco-Welsh alliance began when the cloths were drawn and the diners sat at their ease over piments of hippocras, wine spiced with cinnamon, ginger, cardamon and nutmeg served with wafer biscuits. The envoys were a great success with the Court, ever eager for novelty. Charles questioned them closely about their prince. When Hanmer told him that his brother-in-law's main interest was soldiering, the king presented him with a gilded helmet, breastplate and sword to take back with him to Owain.

In this atmosphere negotiation prospered. On June 14, after a heady month of receptions and banquets, the king appointed the Bourbon Earl of March and John, Bishop of Chartres, to conclude an agreement with the envoys of the 'magnificent and mighty Owain, Prince of Wales'. Owain had come a long way from the parliament which had dismissed him as a 'barefoot, Welsh scrub'.

Another month of tournaments and feasting followed whilst the terms of the treaty were drawn up. At last the ground work was done, and in the Paris home of Arnaud de Corbie, the Chancellor of France, the treaty was signed. Hanmer and Young signed for Wales. For France the signatories were the Earl of March, his brother Louis the Count of Vendome, Chancellor Corbie, Philip the Bishop of Noyon, Peter the Bishop of Meaux and John, Bishop of Arras. The treaty was a triumph for the Welsh envoys and on their return Owain lost no time in publishing its terms to his parliament:

'In the first place that the said lords, the king and the prince shall be mutually joined, confederated, united and leagued by the bond of a true covenant and real friendship and of a sure, good and most powerful union against Henry of Lancaster adversary and enemy of both parties, and his adherents and supporters. Again that one of the said Lords shall desire, follow and will ever procure the honour and advantage of the other and should any damage or injury intended against the one by the said Henry, his accomplices, adherents, supporters or others whatsoever come to the notice of one, he shall prevent that in good faith. The one, also of these, shall urge and make with the other each and every thing, which by good, true and faithful friends ought to be urged and done to a good and faithful friend, yielding to no-one by fraud or guile. Again, if and as often as the one of them shall know or shall understand that any injury or damage is procured or plotted against the other by the aforesaid Henry of Lancaster or by his adherents or supporters he shall, as many times as it shall become necessary signify that fact and shall advise him concerning and over that so that the other shall be able to prepare against his malice as far as he shall have foreseen. Also, both of the same

lords without distinction, shall be anxious to hinder the aforesaid injury or damage in good faith.

'Again, if anyone of the said lords be pacified in any manner, if
anyone of his subjects gives, makes or procures aid, advice of any
kind in favour of the said Henry of Lancaster his followers or
adherents, for reward or even without reward, against anyone of
their lords. That if they presume to withstand, they shall be
punished in such manner that shall give an example to others.
Again, that none of the lords, the king or prince aforesaid shall
make or take truce, nor make peace with the aforesaid Henry of
Lancaster but that those others might be included if he had
wished in the same truce or peace . . .

'Again that all the subjects of the kingdom of France with their
ships, merchant or mercenary, chattels and goods whatsoever
shall be taken, collected and surrendered without delay in all the
lands and ports of the kingdom of France, provided that subjects
of every degree have, from this time forth, letters of testimony
under the seal of their lords . . .

'Again that if strife, violence, battle, riot, pillage or other injury
whatever, and may that not happen, be committed or caused to
arise on sea or land, between the subjects of the said lords, and
should a pretext appear over this, let it be treated amicably
according to their merits and extent of places where the offences
were committed, by the lords of both parties or their justiciars or
officers to whom that pertains and that offences of every kind
committed by them shall be legitimately resolved reformed and
the aforesaid lords on his part shall have required of the other he
will be held by his letters to ratify, confirm and even to make valid
with binding promises . . .'

The alliance with France gave Owain the political stature he
needed. He was no longer a rebel, bent only on chasing the
English out of Wales; indeed he had largely achieved that aim. He
was now a very real threat to Henry and an increasingly attractive
prospect in the eyes of the men of power who surrounded the
throne.

John Trevor, the Bishop of St Asaph, was the most important
catch Owain made at this time. Trevor had deserted his first

benefactor, Richard, when he saw power moving to Henry. Now, as Henry's power seemed to decline, Trevor attached himself to a new master, Owain. It must be said that once Trevor joined Owain he served him with devotion until his death six years later in Paris where he was seeking support for Owain's cause. Nor were Owain's successes confined to politics; his military campaigns prospered. By the end of June the Prince of Wales had withdrawn his small force to Worcester leaving North Wales to Owain's rule. A third of Shropshire was laid waste and on June 10 Archdeacon Kingeston was once again writing from Hereford:

'The Welsh rebels in great numbers have entered Archenfield and there they have burned houses, killed the inhabitants, taken prisoners and ravaged the countryside to the great dishonour of our king and the unsupportable damage of the country. We have often advertised to the king that such mischief would befall us, we have also certain information that within the next eight days the rebels are resolved to make an attack in the March of Wales, to its utter ruin, if speedy succour be not sent.

'True it is indeed that we have no power to shelter us except that of Richard of York and his men, which is far too little to defend us; we implore you to consider this very perilous and pitiable case and to pray to our sovereign lord that he will come in his royal person or send some person with sufficient power to rescue us from the invasion of the said rebels. Otherwise we shall be utterly destroyed, which God forbid. Whoever comes will, as we are led to believe, have to engage in battle or will have a very severe struggle with the rebels. And for God's sake remember that honourable and valiant man the Lord of Abergavenny who is on the very point of destruction if he be not rescued.'

The danger in which Hereford was placed worried the Prince of Wales but he was helpless. In a letter to his father he admitted that shortage of money — his gold plate had followed his jewels to the pawnbroker to pay his troops — prevented him from making any effective counter-move. By midsummer the Welsh army was ranging the English border at will, plundering and

killing. Thirty towers and castles and bonfires on every
Shropshire hill did nothing to deter them. In the fields the
peasants gathered the harvest with one eye on the horizon for the
beacon which would warn them of yet another raid. The English
defence crumbled as the unpaid soldiers drifted away from their
uncongenial garrisons and, if this were not enough, in August the
kingdom was threatened from outside. News reached the king
that a French fleet had assembled on the English Channel, their
raised after-castles crammed with men-at-arms. In the event the
French posed no problem. After a long summer of aimless
cruising the Admiral, the Count of March, returned to France
without making a single attempt to land in England. Nor was it
all victory that year for the Welsh. Late in the summer Rhys
Gethin set out on an extended raid at the head of an army of eight
thousand men from Glamorgan, Usk and Gwent. Their target the
prosperous town of Grosmont. In its early stages the raid was a
complete success. The Welsh army marched through Cardiff and
Newport, both towns still smouldering from earlier raids, and
attacked the castles of Caerleon and Usk. They swept down on
Grosmont and were burning and looting when they were
attacked by a smaller force led by the Prince of Wales and his
three closest friends, Talbot, Newport and Greindor. When the
Prince's force rode down on them in the smoking streets of the
town, the Welsh were piling their carts with booty and they were
at a disadvantage. Beaten back by the Prince and his men, the
Welsh retreated to Campstone Hill outside the town where they
attempted to re-group, but they were not given time. In the attack
which followed, the Welsh standard was captured and the bearer,
Ellis ap Richard ap Howell ap Morgan Llwyd, was killed. The
Welsh fought back and after a time their superior numbers forced
the Prince to retreat to Monmouth. Leaving over a thousand dead
on the hill the Welsh pursued the enemy to Trelog Common
between Tintern Abbey and the gates of Monmouth. In this final
encounter the Welsh captured the English baggage train which
the Prince's troops abandoned in their flight to safety. For all
that, the battle had been enough to rejuvenate the dispirited
Prince. From Monmouth that night he wrote to his father:

'... it is well to be seen that victory is not in the multitude of people and this is well shown, but in the power of God and the aid of the Blessed Trinity. Your people held the field and conquered all the said rebels and killed of them according to a fair account in the field to the time of their return from the pursuit some say eight hundred, some say a thousand, being questioned on the pain of death.

'... and such amend has God granted to you for the burning of your houses in the above mentioned town.

'And of prisoners there was taken only one and he was lately a great chieftain among them, and whom I would have sent but that he is not yet able to ride at his ease.'

Though the battle had proved to the prince's satisfaction that God was an Englishman it did little to reassure the commons. Early in 1405 the population of the Lordship of Brecon made their continued loyalty to the crown conditional on the king showing himself able to contain the rebels. All along the border villages were joining to pay protection, not to Henry but to Owain. In August even the Privy Council had to admit his ascendancy. It allowed Edward Charlton, the people of Welsh-pool and the commons of Shropshire to conclude a separate peace with Owain.

But sweetest of all must have been the language the council used to describe Owain's kingdom.

For the first time they called it:

'The Land of Wales'.

VIII

ABASHED IS NOW THE SAXON

T HE TRIPARTITE Indenture which Owain signed in February 1405 was at best a romantic dream. As a workable treaty it was not worth the misapprehensions it was written under.

Its principal architect was the Earl of Northumberland, a man to whom conspiracy was all. The Earl loved a good plot and he had scarcely missed an opportunity to hatch one since he had first put King Henry on the throne. He was essentially an architect of anarchy, but he had proved at Shrewsbury that he had little taste for carrying the hod in the actual building of a new royal house. The indenture was signed in Wales at the house of yet another prelate who had transferred his allegiance to Owain. David of Aberdaron, the Dean of Bangor and a descendant of the Welsh prince Caradoc, managed the transfer more discreetly than most. It was not until 1406 that his change of loyalties was discovered by the Privy Council which hastened to outlaw him.

At best the wordy document which Owain signed and his son-in-law Mortimer signed on behalf of his nephew the Earl of March is useful as a mark of the height Owain had reached amongst the leaders of the day. It divided England and Wales into three kingdoms and gave the signatories tracts of land quite beyond their resources to administer or defend. Predictably, the Earl of Northumberland did not attend the signing ceremony. Lord Bardolf, at the time still one of Henry's trusted counsellors, conducted the negotiations and signed the indenture on the Earl's behalf. The young Earl of March who, as the descendant of Edward III's second son Lionel, Duke of Clarence, had the strongest claim, came off worst in the share-out. He was to receive only the Thames Valley and the South of England, where Henry's support was strongest, as his portion. The Earl of Northumberland was to rule over the whole of the north of England and the north Midlands. Owain's preoccupation with historic precedent is evident in his portion. The boundary of new Wales was to extend along the Severn bank to the north side of Worcester and then to a group of ash trees, now the village of Six Ashes, on the Kinver-Bridgnorth Road. There is a local tradition that six ancient ash trees stood there and these had a special significance to the Welsh. Thomas Pennant in the 18th Century was to write (none too critical of his sources):

'Owain to animate his countrymen called up the ancient prophecy which signified the destruction of Henry under the name of the mole, cursed of God's own mouth. Himself he styled the dragon, the name he used in imitation of Uther Pendragon, whose victories over the Saxons were foretold by the appearance of a star with a dragon underneath which Uther used as his badge and on that account it became a favourite one with the Welsh. On Percy he bestowed the title of lion from the crest of the family; on Mortimer the wolf.'

In the same prophecy Merlin had foretold that at Bridgnorth Ash Trees in the depth of England a great eagle would muster a host of Welsh warriors who would defeat the English. Whether Lord Bardolf appreciated the significance of the ash trees is open to question. But his agreement to allow Owain a large slice of the Midlands, is an indication of how far the land-jealous Percys were prepared to go to cement their alliance with Owain. From the Ash Trees the frontier of the new Wales followed a more prosaic line along the Staffordshire border to the source of the Trent. From there it ran to the source of the Mersey and followed the line of the river to the sea. Though it was a romantic kingdom, the new frontier did give Owain certain military advantages. Not least among these was the castles of Shrewsbury, Chester and Worcester, no small benefit with the Earl of Northumberland for a neighbour.

One vital ingredient was lacking if the Tripartite Indenture was ever to become more than a political dream. One of the Magi was missing. Edmund, the six-year-old Earl of March was still in the custody of Henry IV. A plot was laid to free him.

Edmund and his five-year-old brother Roger had been committed into the care of Constance, the sister of the Duke of York and the widow of the Lord Despencer whose attempt, early in his reign, to poison King Henry had resulted in his being torn to pieces by a Bristol mob. His countess was perhaps not the wisest choice of guardian for two young children. She was a lady of vigorous sexual appetites. At the time the two young boys were put in her care, she was living in open concubinage, to the scandal of the court, with another minor — Edmund Hallow, the Earl of Kent. For reasons of her own she welcomed the plot, which was simplicity itself. While the court was at Windsor, Henry was to be murdered and the Countess — with her son Richard and a large sum of money — was to flee with the young Mortimers to Wales where her tenants in Glamorgan would shelter them and take them to Owain. In its early stages the plan looked like succeeding. Either by gold or by more intimate persuasions Constance prevailed upon the court locksmith to make her a set of duplicate keys to the Mortimers' quarters, and in mid-February the little party was smuggled out of Windsor at midnight by a servant, Richard Milton. At Abingdon, as the excited children watched wide-eyed, the Countess's esquire, Morgan, was despatched to France with premature news of the success of the plot.

Sadly for her the game was nearly over. Warned of the plan while he was at Kensington, Henry rushed to Windsor and sent an armoured party in pursuit of the fugitives. They were caught in a wood outside Cheltenham, after a short, sharp fight in which both sides suffered casualties. The Countess, the children and an attendant John Ogan were captured and brought under heavy guard to London where, on February 17, 1405 the Council opened an investigation into the plot. The first to suffer was the locksmith. His hands were chopped off and for good measure he was beheaded. Trouble began when Constance was called — for she insisted on naming to the startled councillors the man who, she claimed, was the instigator of the plot. And the man she named was none other than her brother, the Duke of York.

Naturally her brother refuted the allegations. His sister answered by calling for a champion to do battle in her name. She vowed, with a fine sense of theatre, that if he were worsted in the lists she would give herself up to be burned alive. An impressionable esquire, William Maidstone, obviously brought up on the chivalrous romances of Christine the Pisan, took up her cause. In the presence of the king he threw down his hood at the Duke's feet. It was an unkind thing to do. The Duke was the fattest man in the court and the art of picking up the hood, as custom demanded, cannot have been easy for him. But he managed it, purpling with the effort, and accepted the challenge.

Henry was in a quandary. Trial by battle was becoming unfashionable and, besides, the Duke's great weight made the proposed encounter impractical — since no horse strong enough to carry him could be found in the royal stables. There was undoubtedly relief on all sides when his cousin, Prince Thomas, acting as peacemaker, arrested the Duke and conveyed him to the safety of the Tower of London. After a few days in his new quarters the Duke changed his defence. Brought back before the council on March 1 he admitted that he knew of the plot, but he insisted that it was he who had helped the king to thwart it.

His story was accepted. Instead of the death sentence he might have expected the Duke merely suffered the loss of his estates. These were considerable. The crown took the Channel Isles and the Isle of Wight, Prince John was granted the York lands on Tyneside and his place as 'Master of the Running Dogs' went to a fitter man, John Waterton, which was probably a relief to the bulky Duke. For a while he was imprisoned at Pevensey Castle under the charge of Sir John Pelham. But by the end of the year, his estates restored by the endlessly forgiving Henry, he was a guest at the wedding of the Earl of Arundel and in December he was back on the Privy Council. His income was reckonned at £20,000 a year.

Constance also lost her estates and had to 'undergo the annoyance of imprisonment at Kenilworth', in the phrase of her judges. It was a temporary annoyance. At the time of her death in 1416 she was once again in possession of her lands and she was buried in state in Reading Abbey. Even the Mortimer children benefited from their escapade. Though they were subsequently kept in close custody their household allowance was substantially increased.

In the end it was only the locksmith who suffered.

† † †

In Chester, unable to mount an effective army to march against Owain, Prince Henry had to content himself with an attempt to stamp out the city's new basic industry, smuggling to the Welsh. The Prince was told that 'Great quantities of horses, cattle and merchandise are being carried to the fairs of Bromfield, Yale and Dyffryn Clwyd'. The crier shouted himself hoarse with warnings but the trade continued. Two commissioners, Thomas and John Alleyn, were appointed to 'keep the passes of Chester to prevent trade with the rebels' and orders were issued by the prince prohibiting the sale of merchandise to the rebels or its transfer to Malpas, twelve miles from the city 'or any foreign market at which rebels are assembled'.

Not all border communities were as well disposed to the Welsh. In the same year William Bromshull, Captain and Keeper of the Queen's Lordship and Castle of Caus on the Welsh side of the Shropshire border, complained of a reprisal raid. He wrote:

'John Gery, Richard Suggedon, Will Dorset Jnr and Richard Smith of Baschurch and others to the number of 100 came in warlike array whilst the tenants were dwelling peacefully on their land. They slew Gruffydd ap Gruffydd and Iorwerth ap Gwyn, villeins, and took from hence Gwenhwyfar, the former wife of Hywel ap Heylyn, her son John and daughter Joanna and several others. With Thomas Cobberley of Shrewsbury they imprisoned them at ransom and wrongfully and violently chased out of the said lordship 100 other tenants.'

That summer of 1405 the war came dangerously close to Owain.

The Castle of Usk was a recurring threat to his supremacy in Monmouth. Local support was not strong and Owain needed a convincing victory in the district to rally the uncommitted to his cause. The defeat of his force at Grosmont, only a few miles away, had done little to advance his reputation in the area. The town of Usk had suffered badly from his raids. In Rome Adam had painted a sorry picture of the plight of high-born nuns at a convent there in a letter to the Pope:

'Owing to the burnings, spoilings and other misfortunes which have been caused by the wars which rage in these parts, or otherwise, this convent has come to such want that unless ready help be forthwith found by your holiness, the sisterhood will be forced to beg for food and clothing, straying through the countryside or to stay in the private houses of friends; whereby it is feared that scandals may belike arise.'

The scourge of war was everywhere in the town but on its rock the castle remained in English hands. To capture it Owain sent the cream of his army. The commanders included his own son Griffith and his brother Tudor. The warlike Abbot of the Cistercian monastery of Llantarnam, John ap Hywel, marched with them. Abbot John was as bold a fighter as any in the Welsh army. But he was also a deeply religious man and as he rode, his gown tucked under his thighs, at the head of the soldiers he worried about the salvation of the men behind him. He saw ample evidence of the distance from grace in which his men stood and by the time the army halted to celebrate the pre-battle mass out of bow-shot of the castle his fear for their souls was overwhelming. He was silent whilst a brother abbot preached a fiery sermon exhorting the soldiers to die bravely. 'Tonight,' the first abbot is said to have promised them, 'you will sup in heaven.'

Abbot John was less sanguine and he used the last moments before the battle to urge repentance.

'Success will die upon you, unless you repent your lives,' he warned the men as they stood before him in their ranks.

Whilst the sermons were being preached the defenders were already preparing. The garrison had been secretly strengthened in preparation for the raid. Horses were led from their stables into the inner court, armoured knights astride with their lances hooked into the rests. Mounted men at arms with swords drawn waited in their ranks and two watchmen stood ready to swing up the great bar that held the castle gate. In the van were Lord Grey of Condor and Sir John Greyndour, knights of proved worth against the Welsh army. At their signal, given at the moment the Welsh began their first wild charge up the hill to the castle, the gates were opened, the drawbridge lowered and the troop of knights rode out to meet them. The Welsh broke and fled in rout. Hunted by the mounted knights they scrambled through the river at the foot of the castle meadows, took to their horses and galloped for the safety of the hill country. Behind them, bent over their lances, swords waving, the royal troops thundered hacking and spearing anyone in their path.

On the hill of Pwll Melyn (The Yellow Pool) the Welsh had barely dismounted and formed into battle lines before the English were upon them. In the slaughter which followed the Abbot of Llantarnam was killed, Tudor Glyndŵr was hacked to death and Griffith Glyndŵr and three hundred Welsh soldiers were taken prisoner. At first when they saw Tudor's body the English believed they had killed Glyndŵr himself. Then a man who knew him pointed out that the corpse lacked the wart which was the distinguishing feature between the two men.

The English led the prisoners back to the castle with Griffith roped in a halter with his men. On the flat land before the castle all three hundred soldiers were beheaded and Griffith was sent under heavy escort to the Tower of London. The mass execution had the intended effect on the local population. Writing a hundred years later the Welsh poet Gwilym Hiraethog recorded:

'1405. A slaughter of the Welsh on Pwll Melyn Mountain near Usk, where Gruffydd ab Owen was taken prisoner. It is now the tide begins to turn against Owain and his men. At this time

Glamorgan made its submission to the English except for a few who went to Gwynedd to their master.'

The rot was not long in spreading. The next year Hiraethog noted that Gower, the Towy Valley and most of Cardigan 'yielded and took the English sides'.

In the *Iolo Manuscripts*, an admittedly dubious collection of early Welsh writings, an anonymous scribe wrote:

'In 1405 a bloody battle attended with great slaughter that in its severity was scarcely ever exceeded in Wales took place on Pwyll Melin; Gryffyth ap Owen and his men were taken and many of them were put to death when captured whereupon all Glamorgan turned Saxon except for a small number who followed their Lord into North Wales.'

But it was Adam of Usk, far away in Rome, who had the most graphic account of the battle in his home town.

'Griffith, the eldest son of Owen, with a great following made assault, in an evil hour to himself, on the castle of Usk which had been put in some condition of defence and wherein were the Lord Grey of Condour, Sir John Greyndour and many other soldiers of the king. For those same lords, sallying forth manfully, took him captive and pursuing his men even to the hill country of Higher Gwent through the river Usk, there slew with fire and the edge of the sword many of them without ceasing, driving them through the monk's wood where the said Griffith was taken. And their captives, to the number of three hundred they beheaded in front of the said castle near Ponfald and certain other prisoners of more noble blood they brought, along with the same Griffith to the king. The which Griffith being held in captivity for six years, at last in the Tower of London was cut off by pestilence.'

While Griffith was being led off to captivity and death his defeated army was making its way back through the mountains to North Wales. Amongst them was the bellicose abbot who had exhorted the Children to fight bravely. Mockingly a soldier asked him why he had not stayed to share the heavenly banquet he had promised for the valiant dead.

'Alas, my son,' the abbot is said to have replied, 'today is one of my fast days.'

Perverse as ever, the English parliament was unimpressed by the victory. In November they complained about the war in Wales; they accused the king of doing nothing to end it. They complained about the French, about royal expenditure, about everything they could think of. Yet the blow which Owain had received was considerable. The defeat at the Yellow Pool had robbed him not only of his brother and his eldest son; it damaged his reputation as a leader. The subsequent defection of great areas of South Wales to the English crown showed how frail his newly won kingdom was and other desertions from his kingdom were inevitable. Though North Wales was fully committed to him his power was fading in the rest of the country. Whatever the reaction of parliament, Henry himself was in no doubt that a crippling blow had been dealt to the Welsh. A new success in Anglesey at Rhosymeirch had led to the recapture of Beaumaris Castle, for some time in rebel hands. This meant the island was no longer a safe refuge for the Tudor brothers and they moved their headquarters across the Menai Straits to the Snowdon Mountains. So inviting was the prospect of overthrowing Glyndŵr that the king overcame his distaste for campaigning in Wales and began to plan a final expedition into the country. With sudden energy he bullied parliament into granting him funds and rode to Hereford to command what he profoundly hoped would be the last Welsh campaign.

Yet again the Commissioners of Array were sent off and the young men of the towns and villages paraded before them for selection. Victuals were assembled. In small farms and cottages all over the Midlands the women worked the fields, while the men sharpened weapons, polished breast plates and stuffed the inside of their helmets with strips of cloth for comfort. Horses were led from their stables to be entered on the army rolls and assessed for compensation against loss or injury. In the manor houses the clerks drew up new indentures for the knights, whose squires paraded and inspected the mercenaries who would fight under their banners. Patriotism grows strongest when it is fertilised with military success and there was a new confidence in the long columns of men and horses which made their way towards the mustering point at Hereford. The narrow lanes which led to the city were choked with marching men and troops of mounted knights and men-at-arms. There was little artillery in Henry's army but what there was he had brought to Hereford. The gun carriages trundled behind the columns of men, brushing the bushes and snatching at the long boughs of hawthorn blossom which caught in the wheels.

Within the city that May taverns did a roaring trade. From tavern to tavern door, boozed soldiers staggered, their pouches jingling with advance pay, hugging each other for support. The shocked population of the Cathedral City stuffed their ears against the raucous bawdry of their songs. Inside the taverns at low, rough-surfaced wooden tables by tallow light the soldiers sprawled, as they have always done before battles, engaged in wordy wars of their own.

There were watchers in the taverns. They were smaller and darker than the Saxon Countrymen who made up the royal army. They went about the town drinking little but listening and counting. These spies, their lives at risk with every moment they spent in the town, until, dodging through the back streets and scaling the wall, they made their way back across the river to Owain. The news they brought was chilling. The Royal Army now being mounted was a huge force of nearly 40,000 men backed with heavy artillery.

Owain knew that he had no hope of defeating an army of the size which was now coming to muster. His own troops were demoralised by the defeat at the Yellow Pool and he had lost two generals. To meet the army on the Welsh border in open battle, was untenable; yet, to allow it to enter the country unchecked and content himself with sporadic attacks was in his present situation unwise. His supporters in mid-Wales, where the main English thrust would be made, were uncertain in their allegiance. An army of 40,000 would inevitably send them back to the king. Only by diverting the attention of the king and forcing the army to defend itself from an attack from another quarter could Owain hope to save his kingdom. Fortunately an alternative was at hand. John Trevor and David of Aberdaron were in York with Lewis Byfort and the Earl of Northumberland. They had gone to bake the bricks of yet another conspiracy the Earl was building there. A rising by the Northern rebels would force the king to postpone the invation of Wales.

The Scrope Conspiracy was one of the most ambitious of the many plots against the House of Lancaster during the reign of Henry IV. Its titular leader was Richard Scrope, the Archbishop of York, a kinsman of Northumberland and now drawn by him into that arch-plotter's web. The Archbishop, a saintly and unworldly man, had been an early adherent of Henry. He had officiated at his coronation and at the time of the rising in York he was still a member of the Privy Council. Although he agreed that there should be a rising in the North it was in the Archbishop's interest to delay it until the campaign into Wales was well under way. But he was no match for the combined eloquence of Byfort, Trevor and Aberdaron; and the Welsh won.

Once committed, the Archbishop threw himself whole-heartedly into the plot. A scarlet cape over his white linen robe, he strode across the Minster green at York from Bishop's Palace to hammer the rebel manifesto onto the great door of his church. As the townsfolk crowded behind him to read its terms messengers were already galloping over the county, carrying copies of the manifesto scribbled days before by the monks. Other copies appeared all over the city proclaiming the link between the York insurgents and the Welsh. It spoke, in terms, of an alliance with Glyndŵr on whose behalf the Welsh bishops had given a firm undertaking to end their war with England if Henry was overthrown. The manifesto promised 'satisfaction and contentment from those now in rebellion in Wales, peaceful now as they were in Edward III's and Richard II's reign'. Moved by devotion to the Archbishop the populace of York joined his rebellion. When, flanked by his fellow conspirators, Thomas Mowbray, the son of the Duke of Norfolk and Earl Marshal of England and Sir William Plumpton, the Archbishop marched out of York behind a banner displaying the five wounds of Christ, an army of 8,000 fighting men and most of the population of York followed.

The effect on the king was precisely what the Welsh had hoped for. The campaign in Wales was cancelled and by May 28, 1406 the king was in Derby, heading North. News came of a second army of 7,000 rebels raised by disaffected Yorkshire knights from Northallerton, Cleveland and Topcliffe. Its leaders were Sir Ralph Hastings of Slingsby, Sir John Fauconberg of Cleveland, Sir John Fitzrandolph from Middlehan and Sir John Cilvil from Ryedale. The Cleveland rebels were less lofty in their purpose than the religious procession which marched out of York. As it marched south, the Cleveland mob — for it was little more — looted and ravaged the homes of those who would not come out in support.

Once again it was an 'illness' of the Earl of Northumberland which wrecked the conspiracy. He was to meet the men of Cleveland with his supporters on the banks of the River Swale at Topcliffe. Predictably he failed to arrive and the Earl of Westmoreland, galloping south from his border home with a troop of royalist cavalry, was able to drive a wedge between the forces of Cleveland and those of York.

Westmoreland was a Percy. He had none of Hotspur's martial ability but he displayed the family guile when the royalists and the rebels came face to face on Shipton Moor six miles north west of York on the fringe of a wooded marsh, the Royal Forest of Galtres. Although heavily outnumbered the Earl deployed his troops on sloping ground. The York rebels were over-awed by the professionalism of the soldiers who faced them and for three days the two sides watched each other in check-mate. Westmoreland set up his headquarters behind a small hill which obscured it from the rebel view and sent heralds to arrange a

Old Parliament House. (By permission of the Gwynedd Archives.)

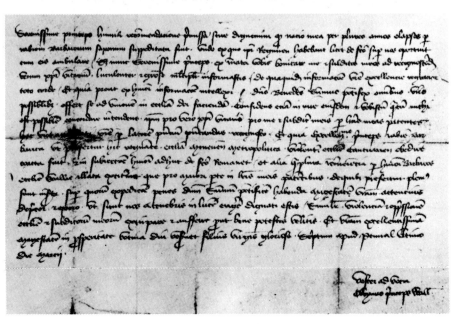

A facsimile of Owen's letter to Charles VI of France, stating the position of the Welsh Church as Owen saw it. (By permission of the National Library of Wales.)

OLD PARLIAMENT HOUSE DOLGELLY

EXTERIOR VIEW.

INTERIOR OF HALL

Old Parliament House. (By permission of the Gwynedd Archives.)

parley with the Archbishop. Scrope believed his promise of safe-
conduct and unfettered negotiation, and with Mowbray and
Plumpton, rode off behind the heralds to Westmoreland's headquarters. The last his army saw of him that day was when he
disappeared from view behind the hill. At his tent Westmoreland
welcomed the party and invited them to take wine with him. A
contemporary wrote of what followed:

'The Earl had bottles of wine and made them drunk. And while
the Earl pretended to treat, a knight of his rode to the Archbishop's host and said the lords had reached an agreement and in
token thereof were drinking together. "And therefore" he said,
"the Archbishop commands every man to go home again for he
shall this night sup with the Earl of Westmoreland."

'The Archbishop's men were afraid, for there was between
them and the archbishop a little hill so they could not see him or
the earl. Nevertheless they dispersed and the knight returned to
tell the Earl who fell upon the archbishop and Lord Mowbray and
took them prisoners to Pontefract.'

It was a blatant violation of 'safe conduct' one of the most
sacred military obligations of the day, but it effectively ended the
Scrope Rebellion. By the time Henry rode into York the rebellion
was over and he was met by the entire population, barefoot and
wearing halters. They fell before him begging royal forgiveness;
and it was granted but there was no forgiveness for the Archbishop. The Welsh bishops and, of course, the Earl of
Northumberland escaped to Scotland but Scrope, Mowbray,
Plumpton and a Welsh knight, Sir John Griffiths, were brought
to trial in York.

The trial of a prelate was without precedent. The Archbishop
was responsible only to Rome and the king had no authority to
try him, much less to order his death. In his dilemma Henry
appealed to Lord Chief Justice Gascoigne, a man whose
knowledge of law was unrivalled but the appeal brought little
comfort to the king for Gascoigne's judgement was unequivocal.

Although the other conspirators could be executed without reproach the Lord Chief Justice refused to pass sentence on the Archbishop. He ruled that neither king nor subject had power over a bishop and he refused to preside over the Bishop's trial. It was a set-back but Henry was determined that there would be a trial which would show that no rebel, however highly placed, was immune from his justice. He offered the job around the judiciary with, at first, little success. Gascoigne's authority was strong in his profession and many lawyers turned down the King's offer before Sir William Fulthorpe of Durham agreed to risk the wrath of the Church. Finally, in the great hall of Bishopthorpe, while the King breakfasted with the Earl of Arundel, the Archbishop and his fellow conspirators were sentenced to the block. Religious opinion throughout Europe was horrified and the Archbishop of Canterbury hurried north to plead for Scrope's life. In an interview with Henry he begged the king not to defile his hands with a prelate's blood but the king was adamant.

'I may not for the uproar of the people,' he replied but one important obstacle to royal 'justice' remained. The royal officers still had to find someone who was prepared to risk eternal damnation by executing an archbishop. At last, in Thomas Alman of Poppleton they found a man whose soul was already in irredeemable pawn to Satan. He was serving fifteen years in York goal and he offered to take on the job in return for a royal pardon.

On the day of his execution Archbishop Scrope asked the king's officers to allow him to ride to his death with dignity, carrying his crozier and wearing the white linen robe of his office. The request was brusquely refused and he was bundled into a scarlet riding cloak with a violet hood. Rough hands lifted him onto the bare back of a blown, old mare with a length of worn rope for a bridle, but they could not steal his dignity. As the condemned party set out for their execution Mowbray, little more than a boy, showed signs of giving way to the fear which all must have felt. Reining in his mare the Archbishop put his hands on Mowbray's shoulders.

'Let us suffer death meekly,' he told him 'for we shall, by God's grace, this night be in paradise.' Throughout the journey to the block the Archbishop was totally composed, even light-hearted. When he recognised anyone in the crowd he acknowledged him gaily. The king's physician, John Malvern, a free-thinker had come to watch the Archbishop die and Scrope saw him.

'We shall have no need of your physic to-day, John,' he called. The doctor could not resist a last theological gibe.

'Perhaps not for the body, but you will need it for your soul,' he shouted back and the Archbishop smiled.

'Come sir and watch me die,' he invited. 'If you see ought against the truth I bow to your correction.'

The block had been set up in a field of young barley outside the south west corner of the walls of York by the Skeldergate. As the procession halted before it, the owner of the field pushed his way through the crowd complaining that his crop would be trampled. The Archbishop offered to kneel for the axe in the road to save the barley but his guard refused; telling the brave old man that no traitor should have the right to choose his place of death. The Earl Marshal died first and next Plumpton while the Archbishop prayed by the block. At last it was his turn and the crowd fell silent. The hollow of the block was already drenched with the blood of Plumpton and Mowbray. The Archbishop knelt before it, folded his arms over his breast and turned to Alman who was standing at his side, the great executioner's axe, its silver rim crimson with blood, held before him.

'For His love that suffered five wounds for all mankind, give me five strokes and I will forgive you all my death.'

It was the only wish that day that was granted to him. It was not until the fifth bloody blow that his head was finally severed and it fell, balancing for a moment on the block's edge, into the basket which contained the heads of his lieutenants.

In Scotland the rebels who had escaped, Northumberland and the Welsh bishops, met with a mixed reception. As refugees of Henry they were sheltered but the Percys had been enemies of Scotland for too long for the welcome to be sustained. After some uneasy months, during which Northumberland tried vainly to see the mysterious madman many still believed was Richard, the refugees learned that the Scots nobles were on the point of handing over Northumberland and the bishops to Henry in return for the Scottish knights taken by Hotspur at Humbleton Hill. The news sent the conspirators galloping back to Wales where they found Owain's court rejuvenated. The Scrope conspiracy had lifted the threat of invasion and Charles VI had ordered an army to be mustered for the invasion of England.

IX

FIRE AND THE EDGE OF THE SWORD

HEN the French invasion of Britain was announced, the young bloods of the realm flocked to join. Estates were mortgaged and old families made bankrupt so that the equipage of the master could out-shine that of his neighbours. The Commanders of the force did little to curb the younger men by example. Jean of Hengest, the Lord of Hugeville, was Master of the King's 600 bowmen. So carried away was he by the prospect of the war before him that he sold his estate at Agencourt, near Mondidier to the Church of Paris to equip his followers.

Jean of Rieux, the elderly Marshal of France, was titular commander but the actual leaders were Robert the One Eye of La Heuze and the Admiral of France Renault of Trie, the Lord of Fontenay, who was to command the invasion armada. The army comprised 800 men-at-arms, each with a suite of squire, page and three archers; the 600 crossbowmen and 1,200 light infantry-men. A fleet of 140 ships was assembled at Brest to carry this socially unimpeachable invasion force across the Channel.

War in France was very much a gentleman's sport, conducted according to the rules of the tournament. To the French knight the horse was all. Neither the crushing defeat by the British bowmen at Crécy, nor the humiliation of the capture of the King of France, John the Good, at Poitiers did anything to alter this view. War was an affair between horsemen of gentle birth and the role of the foot soldier was that of servant. The 'Jacqueries', the French peasantry, lacked the breeding for combat.

By the time the fleet reached Milford Haven from Brest every one of the fine horses had died of thirst. They had not been carrying enough drinking water. But it was a beautifully dressed and noble army.

The first news of the French plans reached Henry from two Welsh spies who had attended the parliament at Harlech Castle at which Owain had announced the French intervention. While the parliament was voting Owain funds to raise a force of 10,000 men Evan ap Maredudd, the Steward of Hope and Langdale and his neighbour David Whitmore of Whitford Llan, were galloping to Chester to give the news to their master, Sir John Stanley. The news was passed to the King at Pontefract Castle and he sent out urgent writs to the sheriffs of eighteen counties.

The writs called on 'all knights, esquires and other fencible men ... hasten to draw to the city of Hereford to march with the king and manfully resist the king's enemies; as now newly it has come to our ears that the Siegneur de Hugevyke and a great number of his other enemies of France with a fleet of ships have landed at Milford Haven to reinforce the Welsh rebels and with them are purposing to invade the realm and the marches of Wales and to do what mischief they may to the king and his lieges'.

For five years Henry had been fighting the Welsh, the Scots and his own nobles. Now once again he set across England to fight a new army of 10,000 Welshmen and a major invasion force of French knights and their followers. At the end of the first year of his reign the exchequer had a credit balance of a little over £24,000 at to-day's values. Since that time there had been heavy inroads on the royal funds, the indentures of his fighting knights had to be renewed and gifts of lands made to propitiate those of his captains who remained loyal to him. Money had poured out to repair castles under constant attack. In August 1405 Henry was all but penniless. Not even the fabulous private fortune his father John of Gaunt had assembled was sufficient to meet his expenses. Every day brought fresh appeals from his son and his chief officers to meet the arrears of soldiers' pay. His threadbare army was in no condition to oppose determined invasion, yet somehow it always did.

In contrast, the French when they landed at Milford Haven made a brilliant show. At a time when the armourers of Milan were the finest in the world, the French wore Italian armour. The pouches and coffers of the French 'tourists' were bursting. Watched by Welshmen who had been pillaged and robbed for five years and whose crops had been burned, the French visitors drank fine wines at magnificent banquets.

After they had bought remounts to replace the horses lost on the voyage the French began their invasion boldly. They slaughtered every inhabitant of Haverford they could find and wasted the country round the town, although they failed to capture Haverford Castle which was successfully defended by the Earl of Arundel. At Tenby the 10,000 strong Welsh army was waiting for the French but it cannot have been encouraged by their next move. A fleet of thirty English fighting ships commanded by Lord Berkely and Henry Pay, the Warden of the Cinque Ports, had already attacked and sunk a munitions convoy of 14 Frenchmen making for the Welsh coast. Then the fleet appeared in the Haven and sank fifteen of the invasion transports. It was a surprise attack, and the invaders were dismayed. Even partisan French historians writing of the campaign admit that only the sinking of their ships kept the French in Wales.

Rallying his allies Owain marched on Carmarthen which surrendered. Glamorgan was next punished for its defection to Henry and the now restored chivalry marched on Herefordshire, which they laid waste. It was not all battles. The Welsh stories of their early leader Arthur had caught the imagination of the French court and they had built him into their Siegfried, surrounded by a whole cycle of heroic myths. Accordingly, on the march to Worcester, a detour was made to Caerleon so that the knights could inspect the Roman amphitheatre, which at that time was believed to be the original Round Table of the Arthurian Knights. Sadly, the chivalric response which this stirred in the minds of the French nobles did not survive their arrival at the gates of Worcester. In the Middle Ages Worcester, a religious centre of great sanctity, was also a rich market town. From the watch towers above the city gates — Frog, Sidbury, Friars and College — the merchants watched the advance of the Franco-Welsh army with alarm. Their fears were justified. Worcester was the first large English city the French had come upon. Not since the Norman invasion had a foreign army penetrated so far into England and the French made the most of their precedent. Down Anger Lane from the Horse Fair the Worcester citizens fled from their attackers, horses and cattle stampeding before them; down Smock Alley to the burial ground of the Black Friars where they were penned and slaughtered. The Butter and Cheese market at the Grass Cross was looted and labourers waiting for hire were butchered where they stood. The Corn Market was pillaged and frightened women fled through Cokyn Lane, the route down which in more peaceful times scolds were dragged for their ritual duckings in the River Severn. When at last the invaders, baggage carts piled with loot, marched out of the city Worcester was a smoking ruin. In high spirits the army made its way through the Shire.

One of the great imponderables of this bizarre invasion is why the invading army chose to camp on Woodbury Hill. Certainly it is a fine defensive position; from the top of its twenty seven acres it commands the horizon in every direction. From the Bristol Channel on one side and deep into the heart of England on the other, the countryside for miles around can be seen from the summit. Four men could prevent surprise attack from any point of the compass and the hill has been a fort for centuries. Even today, jostled by butterflies, it is possible to trace a defensive ditch with a formidable earth embankment which early British warriors dug round the cupped and lightly wooded summit. Only determined and dangerous frontal assault up the slopes of the hill could bring about its capture. It was emminently defensible but the invaders were not in a defensive situation. If they were intending serious invasion they should have marched on. If they were merely raiding and had reached the limit of their plan they should have returned to Wales before the English army could come upon them. To set up camp as they did on the summit of Woodbury Hill was folly. However rich their spoils from Worcester they could not feed 15,000 men for any length of time in a siege, and the problems of supply were insoluble. Whilst an attacking army could not hope to take the summit it was an obvious tactic to blockade it and there is no water supply on the summit of Woodbury.

When Henry arrived with his army he had only to take up a position across the valley on the northern slopes of Abberley Hill to checkmate the invasion. Abberley and Woodbury form the tip of a crescent of hills with a wide, flat valley between them. Henry's lines of supply went through friendly country to Hereford; the country round the Franco-Welsh force was hostile. In order to break the impasse the French would have to leave their safe summit thus surrendering the advantage of ground to Henry. In their confusion the thoughts of the French turned, typically, to the tournament.

Great Whitley, which stands between the two hills, is the most improbable village that can be imagined. It has two coal depots, a hotel on a breath-taking site, very few houses, the most magnificent baroque church in England and the spectacular ruin of a stately home. But in all its unlikely life it can never have witnessed a situation so bizarre as that which unfolded that August. Every morning the soldiers were called to arms. Then on either hill, the two armies were able to watch the jousting knights of both sides engage in formal bouts of armed combat below them in the valley.

The French knights, superb horsemen, rode down a natural tunnel from Woodbury whilst from Abberley, attended by their squires, the English knights rode to meet them. The flat land between the hills was a natural tilt yard. The contests began with formal challenges. The names and achievements of each knight were exchanged and defiances made before individual bouts began. Then, lances couched, helmeted heads low over the necks of their horses to reduce the size of their target, the knights galloped at each other across the green valley floor. During the eight days that this military stalemate continued some of the noblest of the French were killed. The Bastard of Bourbon, Patroullors, the brother of the Admiral de Tries the Lord of Martellons and the Lord of the Valle all died on the tip of an English lance or were hacked to pieces with a sword. In all 200 knights from both sides died in these impromptu sporting engagements.

It was magnificent but it was not war.

Henry tired of the game first. After eight days the invaders woke one morning to find the hill opposite empty of troops. Under cover of night the king had withdrawn his army, marching them under the noses of the sleeping French on Woodbury. Once awake the invaders were soon mounted and galloping in pursuit. They caught up with the royal force at the gates of Worcester and were able to capture eighteen supply wagons before the English found safety behind Worcester's walls. Then it was Henry's turn to pursue as the Welsh led their allies back to Wales. Fighting rearguard actions the French at last reached the coast where they embarked in the fleet which was to take them ignominiously home. The invasion was over. A force of 1,700 Frenchmen did remain behind but they became a source of major embarrassment to their hosts. In the hard winter which followed the majority turned footpad.

The high hopes of the Spring thus ended in disillusion for Owain, yet his achievements had been considerable. No foreign army had penetrated so far into England. With better led allies he might well have reached London. It is tantalising to speculate what Hotspur might have done with a reinforcement of 10,000 Welshmen.

Certainly there was considerable opposition to the House of Lancaster in the country as later the same year a scandal once again touched one of the king's trusted aides.

The first rumblings of the storm were heard in the unlikely surroundings of a country assize. John Oke of Newent in Gloucestershire had stolen sheep, horses, and lambs all over Essex and Berkshire from 1401 until 1404, but at last his luck deserted him and he was locked in the dungeons below Huntingdon Castle facing an almost certain death penalty. He had admitted stealing five horses, valued at 100 shillings from John Ynge at Wantage in Berkshire and to Sir Paganus Tiptoft, the Sheriff and John Benyll, the king's coroner for the county, it looked like being yet one more dull petty examination of an offender. But John Oke had another crime to confess which brought him squarely into the centre of political events. He claimed that he had been an agent for Owain Glyndŵr, employed to collect funds from English religious houses which were financing the rebellion. A second prisoner, John Veyse of Holbeach in Lincolnshire who had been in prison with Oke on similar charges, confessed that he too had been an agent and fund collector for Owain. Tiptoft and Benyll were in a difficult situation. The device of criminals to escape the death penalty by turning informer was familiar to them. But Oke named twenty-seven land-owners and churchmen whom he accused of sending over half a million pounds to Owain. Amongst them the Abbots of Bury St Edmunds, Warden, Woburn and Lavendon. The Priors of Huntingdon, Newenham, Thetford, and Ixworth also appeared on the list he produced at his examination. Veyse added the Abbots of Louth Park, Thorney and Crowland and the Priors of Spalding and Huntingdon to the total. But it was Oke who made the most sensational charge.

He claimed that the man who organised his fund-raising tours and who had received the money on Owain's behalf was a trusted officer of the crown, even then active in the campaign against the Welsh, Sir John Skydmore. It was a pretty dilemma for the two law officers. It was one thing to accuse clerics who were anyway unpopular; an accusation against a powerful land-owner who had the ear of the king was fraught with hazard. Although his brother Philpot had been an early adherent of Owain's, Sir John's loyalty to Henry had so far been beyond question. He had been a member of one commission to investigate rebel activity in Abergavenny, Herefordshire and the Welsh Marches and his industry had secured him a place on a second which was seeking reconciliation with the rebels in the Middle and Southern Marches. He was Constable of Carmarthen Castle and he had been on the king's personal staff during the campaign in Wales in 1404. Under the circumstances Tiptoft's decision to do nothing was understandable. It was not until the royal justices arrived with the commission of gaol delivery on December 8 that news of the conspiracy reached Henry's advisers. Warrants for the arrests of the clerics were issued and the trials which followed created a sensation. Scribes attended from a number of monasteries and they have left vivid, if partial, records. Tiptoft's indictment charged that Oke had admitted:

'... receiving from John Dunhead, jnr. a traitor at London in the church of St Paul on the feast of the Nativity of St John the Baptist (24 June, 1404) 100 pounds of gold and silver which he gave him to take to Owain Glyndŵr, which immediately after the said feast he bore to Owain in Wales, according to John Dunhead, and delivered to the soldier John Skidmore, Owain's receiver at Brecon to sustain the wars, whereof he stands accused.'

Other names followed: 'Walter the Rector of All Saints Church, Huntingdon . . . John Hervy of Melbourne, Cambridgeshire, John Odle, Meldreth, Cambridgeshire, John Copegrave, at Gloucester, John Sabrisford of Huntingdon, John Graunt, Rector of Olney, Bucks'.

But it was the activities of Sir John which interested the court. Oke claimed that he had taken the money from twenty-six collections to him at rendezvous in the Southern March and south-west Wales, an area in which the knight had extensive estates. On one occasion, Oke alleged, he had even visited Skydmore in the royalist stronghold of Powis Castle and on another at Beaumaris Castle while the garrison was fighting off a rebel attack.

Veyse's testimony was, in contrast, a disappointment. His accusations against John Dunwich and the Abbot of Ramsey, John Swyneshead, were summarily dismissed. In the event none of the men accused by the two thieves was found guilty and all were freed. Under a statute which prevented false accusers from benefitting from their accusations Oke and Veyse were drawn from Huntingdon Bridge through the town to the gallows where they were hanged. But the scandal they had started had a longer life. In February 1406 Henry wrote to 'his beloved subject John Cockayn, formerly one of the justices at our goal in Huntingdon charged with the hearing of trials'. He instructed him:

'Knowing of the accusations of John Veyse of Holbeach and Thomas Oke, deceased, former prisoners at Huntingdon gaol, against Thomas, Abbot of Louth Park and John, Prior of Spalding, we order you to hear these charges and all other charges relating to them'.

Over the next two years the king, still suspicious, ordered no less than six enquiries into the testimony of the hanged thieves. There is no documentary proof that Sir John was a traitor to the crown but there are significant pointers. His brother was a known rebel. Sir John had visited Owain Glyndŵr under truce while he was Constable of Carreg Cennen Castle and it is possible that both he and his brother (the one openly, the other secretly) were sympathisers. But perhaps the most significant indication came in 1414 when, after the death of his first wife, Sir John took a new bride. She was Alice Glyndŵr, Owain's daughter.

Certainly Sir John seems to have fallen from royal favour. After the Oke case his family documents abound with suits against him for extortion, sales of office and contempt of the king's rights. In the reign of Henry V, when John Beaufort, Earl of Somerset who had been given the Glyndŵr lands, was taken prisoner by the French, Sir John ungallantly used the opportunity to petition for the return of the estate. In the political infighting which followed he was dismissed from all offices and lost the Constableship of the castles of Kidwelly, Carmarthen, Monmouth and Three Castles. Henry IV's sweetest quality, the capacity for forgiveness was not inherited by his heir.

X

A FURY OF BARBAROUS SAXONS

A LOST OPPORTUNITY and two events over which he had no control cost Owain Glyndŵr his kingdom.

In Scotland Robert III, lame, religious and no soldier, had lost the struggle for power to his brother, the Duke of Albany. The heir to the crown, David, the Duke of Rothesay, had become involved in a plot to assassinate Albany. He was betrayed by one of his drinking companions Sir John Ramorgny. Albany persuaded the king that his son, a noted debaucher, should be placed under restraint. The king, sick and confused, agreed and Rothesay was seized and imprisoned first in the Castle of St Andrews and later at Faulkland Castle where two of Albany's henchmen, Wright and Selkirk, set about starving him to death. For a while Rothesay was kept alive by a woman servant of the castle who, hearing his screams, fed him with barley cakes and her own milk, passed down a pipe. But Selkirk and Wright discovered what she was doing and had her removed and succeeded so well in their scheme that after his death it was discovered that Rothesay had gnawed the flesh from his own shoulder.

Fearing for his other son James, the 14 year-old Earl of Carrick and the new heir, Robert arranged to have him put in the care of the King of France. Accompanied by a heavy escort commanded by the Earl of Orkney, James went to North Berwick where a ship was waiting in the Bass to take him to France. There is little doubt that it was Albany, restless for total power, who told Henry IV of the king's plans for his son, for an armed merchantman from the Wye captured the ship and the Prince off Flamborough Head. At their first interview the Earl of Orkney handed Henry a letter from King Robert, imploring him if bad weather should force his son into an English port to treat him kindly. The Earl told Henry that James was going to Paris for his education.

'I speak French as well as Charles or the Duke of Orleans,' Henry is said to have replied. 'His father could not have sent James to a better master.'

Robert died shortly afterwards and Albany became regent while James spent his youth in the Tower of London, falling in love and becoming a poet in the process. He was well treated and thanks to his presence Henry had one less in his theatre of war to engage him, one less frontier to guard. The threat to Wales increased in ratio.

France remained a danger but a year later this enemy, too, was thrown into confusion when the assassination of the Duke of Orleans robbed Owain of his most eloquent and powerful supporter in the French Court. Burgundy and Orleans had been at odds for years in the struggle for power in France. The followers of the Duke of Burgundy carried on their lance pennons the motto 'I have possession' and those of Orleans 'I envy him'. When the old Duke of Burgundy died he was succeeded by his son John and a new motto appeared on the pennons. It was 'Without Fear'.

The old Duke had been regent of France during the minority of Charles VI but the liaison between Orleans and the Queen had eroded his power. The new Duke decided that Orleans must die.

On the Feast of St Clement, November 23, 1407, after dining in Paris, Orleans went to console the Queen, mourning her baby who had died in childbirth. Unknown to either, some days before the visit eighteen of Orleans's followers led by Raoul d'Augelonville, had taken rooms at 'Our Lady', a nearby tavern. When the Duke arrived the Burgundians sent one of the king's servants, Thomas of Courthouse with a message summoning him to the palace. Normally Orleans travelled with a bodyguard six hundred strong, but on this occasion he had only five link-men and two pages, riding one horse, when he set off to the King. The

Burgundians leapt out of the shadow of a building by the Porte Barbette. Orleans was dragged from his saddle, his hand was chopped off at the wrist and his head smashed with pole-axe blows, until his brains leaked into the roadway. A page who threw himself across the Duke's body was also hacked in pieces.

Owain's hopes of further French help died with the Duke in a Paris gutter, but Henry seized the opportunity to begin new negotiations with the French. In 1405 Owain had ruled all Wales and the English had held the Marches between Chester and Hereford with difficulty. Within four years English domination spread over the south and the central highlands of Wales, until Owain's kingdom in South Wales had shrunk to a narrow, coastal strip which ended short of Cardigan. He was still a formidable opponent. After the retreat from Worcester the people of Pembroke still held him in sufficient awe to offer him £2,000 in silver for a six months truce, but his luck was changing. On St George's Day in 1406 a thousand of Owain's soldiers, including another of his sons, were killed in a battle with Edward Charlton and his levies from Cheshire and Shropshire.

Until 1406/7 Henry had been fighting a war on four fronts. Like the boy on the dyke he had rushed from wall to wall of his kingdom defending it in turn from the Scots, the Welsh and the French. Troubles in Ireland had meant costly expeditions and French privateers disrupted his mercantile trade. A strong and concentrated alliance by his enemies must have ended by his overthrow. Alone among them Owain and his cabinet of shrewd prelates had seen this and they had worked constantly to bring it about. But the myopic policies of Charles of France and Robert of Scotland and the unharmonious confederacy of Irish chieftains brought each attempt to nothing. Scots invasions degenerated into badly led, ill-timed cattle raids; the French concern with personal aggrandisement and the trappings of chivalry had resulted in the pathetic promenade to Worcester. In Ireland harmony between the ruling families would scarcely have survived the boat journey to England. Only in Wales had there been a conception, and that faint and uncertain, of a wider strategy than mere robbery and reprisal. Twice rebel forces had

'The Rout of Owain Glyndŵr's army' from 'Life of Richard Beauchamp' by John Rous. (By permission of the British Library.)

Sion Kent: from a panel at Kentchurch Court. (By permission of J. Lucas-Scudamore.)

been in major confrontations with an English army forced to defend its own land. At Shrewsbury missed opportunity and faint hearted conspirators had saved the crown and at Worcester the campaign had ended in disarray and flight.

Opportunities had been lost and finally fate had neutralised Scotland and France. The English war machine, a basically efficient and highly professional apparatus could be directed solely on Wales. Perversely it was under the threat of ultimate defeat that the noblest of Owain's designs was formed. The schism of the popes earlier in the century produced two contenders for the papal throne, Gregory XII in Rome and Benedict XIII, Charles VI's candidate, in Avignon.

To Owain's court in Harlech came two envoys from the Court of France—Maurice Kerry and a friar, Hugh Eddouyer — bringing a letter from Charles seeking the support of Owain for Benedict. Owain's hopes of further aid from France were indivisible from support for an Avignon Pope but there were problems. Both his Bishops, Byfort and Trevor, were appointees of Rome. England, loyal to Gregory, would insist on their replacement if their contestant won, only the ambitious Young could hope for personal advancement from an Avignon victory. Young has been given credit for the Grand Design which Owain submitted as the price of his allegiance, yet it embodied proposals which in a crude form Owain had been advocating since the early days of his revolt against England. These proposals sought a complete reorganisation of the church in Wales. St David's was once again to become a metropolitan church, only Welsh speaking prelates and clergy were to be appointed and Welsh churches were to be removed from the control of English monasteries, thus restoring the immunities they had enjoyed before the Welsh conquest. Most important Owain wanted the creation of two universities, one in North Wales and the other in the South. It was to take more than 400 years for his plan to mature. He saw that if Wales was ever to achieve nationhood, native seats of learning where Welsh-born administrators could be trained were essential. In the fifteenth century the only higher education available to Welsh scholars was in England or on the continent.

Welsh lawyers, including Owain himself, were trained in England. Canon law was taught at Oxford and all other branches of the legal profession received their instruction at the Inns of Court in London.

His letter to Charles is a masterpiece of diplomacy. Since it speaks with the rare, authentic tones of Owain it is worthy of repeat in detail.

'Most Serene Prince,
    You have deemed it worthy on the humble recommendation sent, to learn how my nation for many years now elapsed has been oppressed by the fury of the barbarous Saxons; whence because they had the government over us and indeed, on account of that fact itself, it seemed reasonable with them to trample upon us. But now, most serene prince you have in many ways, from your innate goodness informed me and my subjects very clearly and graciously concerning the recognition of the True Vicar of Christ. I, in truth, rejoice with a full heart on account of that information of your excellency and because, inasmuch from this information I understand that the Lord Benedict, the supreme pontifex, intends to work for the promotion of a union in the Church of God with all his possible strength. Confident indeed of his right, and intending to agree with you as far as is possible for me I recognise him as the True Vicar of Christ, on my own behalf and on behalf of my subjects by these letters patent, forseeing them by the bearer of their communications in your Majesty's presence.

'And because most excellent prince the Metropolitan Church of St David's was, as it appears, violently compelled by the barbarous fury of those reigning in this country, to obey the Church of Canterbury and de facto still remains in this subjection. Many other disabilities are known to have been suffered by the Church of Wales through these barbarians which for the greater part are set forth fully in the letters patent accompanying. I pray and sincerely beseech your majesty to have these letters sent to my Lord the Supreme Pontifex, that as you deemed worthy to raise us out of darkness into light, similarly you will wish to extirpate and remove violence and oppression from the church and from my subjects as you are well able to. And may the son of the glorious virgin long preserve your majesty in the promised prosperity.

'Dated at Pennal the last day of March 1406.

'Owain, Prince of Wales.'

Charles was delighted and again sent rich gifts to the 'dread Owain' but they did not include the army of which Wales was so desperately in need. Owain was at bay, he and his son-in-law Mortimer still held Harlech Castle and Rhys the Black held a second castle further down the coast at Aberystwyth. Then in the summer of 1407 Prince Henry appeared at the mouth of the Rheidol river at the head of a great force to attack Rhys the Black. The Duke of York, now fully restored to favour, the Earl of Warwick who had captured Glyndŵr's standard, John Talbot, a consummate soldier at the beginning of his long, distinguished career and John Greyndor who had fought and beaten the Welsh at Grosmont, were among the Prince's formidable army of commanders. The huge king's 'gonne' which weighed 4? tons was brought from Pontefract Castle, with an ammunition train of 538 lbs of powder, 971 lbs of salt petre and 303 lbs of sulphur. This 'gonne' and six more from the battery at Pontefract were dragged overland to Bristol and from there by sea to Aberystwyth. Thomas, Lord Berkely, and a battalion of carpenters and engineers brought timber from the Forest of Dean to build the siege engines which would batter at the castle walls and the great towers from which bands of archers could overlook the inner court of Aberystwyth.

When the Prince offered a treaty Rhys had to agree. The train of artillery, a new and frightening development in warfare, must have been daunting. Cut off as they were from supplies the alternative to an honourable peace was death, and the terms Henry offered were generous. He proposed an immediate truce which was to last until October 24 when fighting would be resumed until November 1. If during that period the castle was not relieved Rhys the Black agreed to march out with indemnities and free pardons for himself and his followers. In return Rhys agreed not to damage the castle or town during the period of the truce 'nor seize any ships driven into port by stress of weather and to deliver up all instruments of war including French cannon'.

In pledge of their honour both leaders took the sacrament together before retiring to their commands. True to his word the Prince raised the siege and marched with his men to Hereford leaving a token force of 120 men-at-arms and 360 archers in quarters at Ystrad Fflur. So delighted was King Henry at the news that he overcame his dislike of the country and planned a final progress in Wales in October.

Owain was furious when he heard that Rhys had signed a treaty with Prince Henry and he threatened to behead his commander the day the castle was lost. His anger was understandable. The fall of Aberystwyth would leave the English army free to concentrate its whole offensive on Harlech. Riding to the castle during the period of truce he went through the pantomime of demanding that Rhys should surrender the castle to him. It was at best a delaying tactic. Inevitably in the end Aberystwyth was reduced and captured and the whole weight of the English offensive was concentrated on Harlech.

There are no records of the siege of Harlech and no dates have survived of the day it began, of how long it lasted or when it ended but of its severity there can be no doubt. It did not end until the greater part of the garrison was dead from starvation. All the military strength from Aberystwyth and all the artillery which had been brought so laboriously from Pontefract were now assembled before the barbican of Harlech.

The English had marched from Aberystwyth by the fast coastal route. Frantically Owain prepared his defences. Garrison pioneers dug trap ditches to the east of the castle, beyond its outer defences. Pits were dug, covered with boards and camouflaged with squares of living turf which would collapse beneath the weight of siege engines and assault towers. In high grass thousands of caltrops — spiked iron balls — were scattered, to pierce the hooves of horses or the foot of any man-at-arms who trod on them. The work of provisioning was begun long before

Aberystwyth fell. Barrels of fresh water had been rolled over the drawbridge to forestall the diversion of the culverts which brought fresh water to castle wells. Other barrels were filled with wax, which according to Christine the Pisan, was recommended by Aristotle for making salt water sweet. There were barrels of vinegar for mixing with water to give the defenders vigour when the supply of wine ran out. On the high walks behind the battlements, stood jars of oil, pitch and sulphur and there were more jars filed with lime and heaps of sand beside the murder holes above the portcullis gates. Heated and poured down on men-at-arms the sand would work its way beneath armour — a painful irritant. Lime was more deadly. Christine explains 'When thrown and scattered from walls it enters the eyes of attackers and causes them to be rendered blind.'

By the castle forges stood mounds of old iron which were heated and dropped onto the attackers. There were iron-bound bundles of faggots to be set alight and dropped over the walls by crane on to the enemy. The 'wolf', a crude mechanical rope-operated grab, was hoisted into a tower to be used to catch the piston arm of a battering ram, hoisting it away from the castle walls. Round the inner perimeter of the castle shallow bowls of water were placed and huge cauldrons of accumulated urine and sea water. A ripple on the surface of the shallow pots would give warning of tunnelling beneath the walls. The huge pots of urine were then poured down counter-shafts to drown the enemy miners.

At last the preparations were over and the garrison in the castle awaited the arrival of the enemy. When the English force of a thousand troops arrived they watched from the towers and the embattled boulevards whilst out of bow-shot English pioneers erected the shanty town protected by a high palisade within which the besiegers would live. Inside the palisade were the tent pavilions of the nobles, the camp kitchens and the make-shift taverns. The high fence was designed to protect the besiegers from night patrols from the castle. It also protected the carpenters as they built the siege engines from the timber the army had dragged with it. These were *malvoisins*, 'the bad

neighbours' which soared above them, topping even the castle
walls so that archers on the top platforms had a clear field of fire
into the inner court of Harlech. Below the archers was a rickety
room with a drawbridge door in which men-at-arms hid. When
the door was dropped it bridged the battlements and the men-at-
arms charged out to take the walls. At the foot of each *malvoisin*
were other rooms where miners waited until they were near
enough the walls to start their tunnels.

'Havoc' was cried, the order which sent mounted troops out to
pillage the country round, burning the few crops which remained
standing — for sieges were normally laid just before harvest —
driving the peasants' cattle into army pounds to alienate the
population round the castle. Prisoners taken on raiding parties
had their arms chopped off so that they could no longer bear
arms, then they were driven back into the castle, useless sharers
of the defenders' food supplies. Even the corpses of dead soldiers
and animals were put to use. Catapults hurled them over the
castle walls so that their rotting bodies would spread disease
amongst the garrison.

The siege began formally with a demand to surrender the
castle. It was refused and the archers advanced over the broken
ground before the East front of the castle. Elsewhere the castle
rock is sheer and on the western side it drops giddily to the sea.
Even the eastern front represents a formidable challenge
protected by an outer wall, a wide moat and the barbican. Within
bow-shot the archers halted, bows were drawn and the first hail
of arrows sang between the battlements. Under this covering fire
pioneers rushed out, probing the ground for the traps and the pits
the Welsh had dug. Safe routes charted, the pioneers were set to
work levelling a path over which the engines were dragged by
men and horses. It was hazardous work. From the corner towers
of the east wall of the castle archers could cover the entire length
of the wall with a steady cross-fire of arrows. Foot soldiers in the
first attack who survived long enough to climb the walls on make-
shift ladders lost hands, chopped off at the wrist by defenders as
the English grappled to prevent the ladder from being pushed
from the walls. Miners worked sheltered under mantlets, huts

roofed with the bloody skins of newly killed animals, still wet to
quench the shower of red hot iron and blazing faggots from the
walls.

Siege warfare was always savage and there was little place in it
for chivalry. Waged by experts — and Prince Henry and the
Talbots had few rivals — there was little hope for the besieged
garrison, particularly in Harlech without hope of relief.
Inevitably the day came when supplies ran out but still the Welsh
held on. They held on without water and they still fought when
the last bundle of faggots had been dropped, the last iron heated.

In their misery they were pounded by the royal artillery until at
last, his supporters dying before his eyes, Owain was forced to a
decision. When the garrison was no longer able to withstand
attack, with his son Meredith and a small band of followers he
escaped. His wife Margaret, two of his daughters, one of them the
Lady Mortimer whose husband had died of starvation, her
daughters and her son Lionel surrendered to the royal forces.
Grandmother, mother and children were sent to join Griffith in
the Tower. In 1413, worn out by sickness Catherine Mortimer
and two of her daughters died and were buried in St Swithin's
churchyard. The fate of Margaret Glyndŵr and the other captives
is unknown. In 1413 they were still alive but they were in want.
The crown allowed only £30 a year for their upkeep.

With classic mis-timing, Adam of Usk chose this moment to
return to Wales. In Rome the Lancaster King of Arms had
warned him that his friendship with the Earl of Northumberland
and the disparagements of his rivals had made the king's
indignation 'wax stronger every day'. But Adam was expert at
closing his eyes to unpleasant facts and he was prey to a powerful
temptation. The Pope in Rome had offered him the See of
Llandaff and Adam was never a man to refuse a bishopric.

He wrote: 'I made declaration before the same king of arms
that I would feign myself Owain's man and with my following
would cross over into Wales unto him; and thence, taking my
chance, I would steal away from him to my Lord of Powis, to await
under his care the king's favour.'

It was an appalling misjudgement but Adam was overjoyed at

his own cleverness.

'And so it came to pass. And this declaration saved my life. Snares were laid for me by sea; and eight ships of Devon chased me for two live-long days, and again and again I was hunted like a hare by so many hounds.

'But at last, through the prayers of St Thomas of India whom I beheld in a vision praying to God that he would bless me, I escaped to the port of St Pol de Leon in Brittany; and there in the chapel of St Theliau, where too he slew a dragon one hundred and twenty feet in length, committing myself to his care I daily celebrated mass.

'At length, taking my chance, I landed in Wales at the port of Barmouth and there I hid in the hills and caves and thickets, before I could come to my said Lord of Powis, because he had taken a wife in the parts of Devon, the daughter of the Earl of that name; sorely tormented with many great perils of death and capture and false brethren, and of hunger and thirst, and passing many nights without sleep for fear of the attacks of foes. Moreover on behalf of the said Owain, when it was found out that I had sent to My Lord for safe conduct I was laid under the close restraint of pledges. But, at last, when my Lord was come again into his own and I had gotten from him letters of leave to come unto him and to rest safe with him I got me by night and in secret unto him at his castle of Pool.'

Adam's troubles were not over. He confessed:

'There in the parish church of the same, not daring to pass outside his domain, like a poor chaplain only getting victuals for saying mass, shunned by thankless kin and those who were once my friends, I led a life sorry enough . . .'

Owain meanwhile with his captains Philip Hanmer, Philpot Skydmore, Rhys Griffiths of Cardigan and the Tudor brothers reverted to their guerilla rôle. His chancellor Griffith Young, confirmed now as Bishop of Bangor in place of Byfort who had returned to Rome, remained loyal. They were still a force to be reckoned with. On May 16 1409 the Lords of Ewyas Lacy, Powys,

Oswestry, Gower, Ruthin, Maelienydd, Glamorgan, Pembroke and Abergavenny were ordered back to their castles to suppress further Welsh revolt. Bishop Trevor is mentioned with Owain 'devastating far and wide with their Welsh following, aided by Scottish and French mercenaries'. At about the same time John Talbot was ordered out to seek the Welsh leader. He clearly failed.

On October 17, 1408, in the manor court of Clun on the south west Shropshire border Symkyn Marter was detained at the lord's pleasure on the accusations of Meredith ap Madoc that he sold victuals and arms to the Welsh rebels. In the same court in 1409 the Clerk noted 'one night lately robbers came to the house of David Talrayn against his will for food and drink. He is fined 6s.8d. for not raising the hue and cry'. In the same year John de Ewloe, the Mayor of Chester, was removed from office 'for want of loyalty and tampering with the rebels'. So unsure was the royalist hold on the city that he was replaced by a military governor. In November the Privy Council ordered border lords to 'repudiate truces they had made with Owain to the detriment of the faithful lieges of the crown'.

But the end was in sight. It came first for the Earl of Northumberland who finally met his match for guile. Still plotting, the Earl opened a correspondence with Sir Thomas Rokeby, Sherrif of Yorkshire. Rokeby, though a royalist, duped the Earl into believing he would support a conspiracy. The Earl marched from the Percy lands to Knaresborough in Yorkshire where he was joined by a second conspirator Sir Nicholas Tempest. Rokeby held his troops back until the rebels had crossed the River Wharfe at Wetherby. Then, cutting off their retreat north, he and his troops fell upon them. At 66, despite the precautions he had always taken against just such an eventuality the Earl fell in battle. His henchman Bardolf was taken prisoner only to die of his wounds. The Earl's body was parboiled in a pickle of cloves, cummin and anise, quartered and set up in spikes in York, Newcastle, Berwick and Lincoln where he was as offensive in death as he had been in life.

In 1410 Owain suffered his last major defeat. Rhys the Black,

Rhys Tudor and Philpot Skydmore were sent to Shropshire in command of a large raiding force. At Welshpool they were defeated and all three leaders captured. Rhys the Black was taken to London where he was beheaded and his head spiked on Tower Bridge; Skydmore suffered a similar fate in Shrewsbury and Rhys Tudor was put to death in Chester.

Three years later, worn out by the troubles of his reign, Henry IV fell ill. Gossip of the day claimed that he was sick of leprosy which had appeared as a divine punishment the day after Archbishop Scrope had been put to death. That he was disfigured seems likely. In the last months of his reign he lived in seculsion but by Candlemas he was sufficiently recovered to keep his birthday and he returned to the Palace of Westminster. During a service in the Abbey he fell ill at St Edward's Shrine and he was taken to the Jerusalem Chamber. He rallied sufficiently to ask where he was and he was told. 'It is the end,' he said, 'for I vowed I would die in Jerusalem.' He asked for the Miserere, which contains a special prayer for forgiveness for 'blood guilt', to be sung. He was 47 when he died, worn out by 14 years on the throne.

Henry had refused permission for Richard II's body to be buried near his father, the Black Prince, at Canterbury, but he ordered a tomb there for himself near the shrine of Thomas á Becket, but there was one last grim joke to be played. In the 19th century a manuscript was discovered in a Cambridge library. It was dated 1440 and it was headed 'The Testimony of Clement Maydestone'. It reads:

'Thirty days after the death of Henry IV, September 14th, 1412 (the date is wrong) one of his domestics came over to the House of the Holy Trinity, at Hounslow, and dined there. And as the bystanders were talking at dinner-time of the king's irreproachable morals, this man said to a certain squire named Thomas Maydestone, then sitting at table, 'Whether he was a good man or not, God knows; but of this I am certain, that when his corpse was carried from Westminster to Canterbury by water, in a small vessel, on order to be buried there, I and two more threw his corpse into the sea between Berkenham and Gravesend; for,' he added with an oath, 'we were overtaken by such a storm of winds and waves that many of the nobility who followed in eight ships were dispersed so as with difficulty to escape being lost. But we, who were with the body, despairing of our lives, with one consent threw it into the sea, and a great calm ensued. The coffin in which it lay, covered with a cloth of gold, we carried with great solemnity to Canterbury and buried it. The monks of Canterbury, therefore, say that the tomb of Henry IV not the body is with us as Peter said of Holy David. As God Almighty is my witness and judge, I saw this man and heard him speak to my father T. Maydestone, that all the above was true.

"Clement Maydestone."

The 19th century history in which this story is told reports a curious sequel when the tomb of Henry was opened on August 21, 1842, in the presence of the Bishop of Oxford and Sir Charles Bagot:

'It was found in sawing away part of the wooden coffin that there was also a leaden coffin within it, but so small that the outer coffin had been filled up with haybands which were very sound and perfect. The leaden coffin appeared moulded to the body within it, and on cutting that open the face of the corpse was discovered in perfect preservation; the nose elevated, the cartilege remaining even, though on the admission of air it sank rapidly away. The skin of the chin entire, of the consistence, thickness and colour of the upper leather of a shoe; the beard thick and matted, of a deep russet colour; the jaws perfect, and all the teeth in them except one fore tooth.'

The 19th century historian asks pertinent questions. Was it likely that an outer coffin would be m⁻de so large that it required packing? If so would a royal corpse be packed with hay? The description of the condition of the skin is at odds with every description of Henry's physical condition during the last years of his life. In the hay round the coffin a tiny cross was found. It was made of two twigs tied roughly together, scarcely the sort of cross one would find on a sovereign's breast, the historian concludes persuasively.

Adam of Usk, who was sure the king had been poisoned, recorded that for five years before his death the king had been tormented by 'a rotting of the flesh, a drying up of the eyes and the rupture of his intestine'. If it was Henry in the coffin his physical condition would seem to have improved *post mortem.*

For Owain the years of the legend had begun. Today Wales is honeycombed with caves where he sheltered, like the beds of Queen Elizabeth they are everywhere. One of the most romantic of the legends from this period is contained in the *Iolo Manuscript,* a notoriously unreliable source, but the story is a pretty one. It describes a visit Owain and a companion paid to Sir Lawrence Berkerolles to whom marriage had brought the estates of the ancient Turberville family, including the Castle of Coety:

'Owain Glyndŵr travelled about the country in the guise of a strange gentleman, attended by one faithful friend in the habit of a servant. Both were armed for no unarmed person was secure at the time. Going about to ascertain the disposition of the inhabitants he went to the castle of Sir Lawrence Berkerolles and requested in French a night's lodging for himself and servant which was readily attended by a hearty welcome; the best of everything in the castle being laid before him. So pleased was Sir Lawrence with his friend that he earnestly pressed him to stay for some days observing that he soon expected to see Owen Glyn Dŵr there; for that he had despatched all his tenants and servants, with many other confidential persons, under an oath of fidelity, through all parts of the country to seize Owen, who he was told had come to that district of the principality; and that he was himself sworn to give honourable rewards to his men who should bring Owen Glyn Dŵr there alive or dead.

" 'It would be very well indeed to secure that man," said Owain, "were any persons able to do so." Having remained at Sir Lawrence's castle for four days and three nights Owen thought it would be wise to go his way. Giving his hand to Sir Lawrence he addressed him thus: "Owen Glyn Dŵr as a sincere friend having neither hatred treachery or deception in his heart gives his hand to Sir Lawrence Berkerolles and thanks him for the kindness and gentlemanly reception which he and his friend experienced from him at his castle. He desires to assure him, on oath, hand in hand and hand on hand, that it will never enter his mind to avenge the intentions of Sir Lawrence towards him; and that he will not, as far as he may allow such desires to exist in his own knowledge and memory nor in the minds of any of his relations and adherents."

'Then he and his servant departed; but Sir Lawrence was struck dumb with astonishment and never afterwards recovered his speech; no word henceforth having ever after escaped his lips.'

Poor Sir Lawrence, his enemy was nearer than he knew. His wife Mathilda poisoned him. Says the chronicler: ' . . . where upon she was buried alive, agreeably to the sentence passed on her by the county and the Lord Sir Richard Began'. Her ghost 'Y Lady Wen' (The White Lady) is reputed to haunt her childhood home near St Athans in South Wales.

The chronicles are occasionally lit by examples of Owain's boisterous humour. When he burned down Cardiff and looted the castle he spared Croker Street which contained a Franciscan Friary. To their chagrin the monks had earlier stored their books and plate in the castle.

'How foolish,' Owain told them, 'to trust your goods to such hazardous safe-keeping.'

The most often quoted legend about Glyndŵr has him sleeping with the Children on their arms in a cave on Ogof Dinas in the Vale of Gwent. 'There they will continue,' says the legend 'until England is self-abased and recognising their country's privilege they will fight for the Welsh who shall be dispossed of them no more, until the day of judgement.'

For at least part of the decade which followed his years of success Owain was very much alive. In 1412 he still held Dafydd Gam prisoner and he was powerful enough for a special commission to be convened to negotiate ransom and release. In 1415 Sir Gilbert Talbot of Grafton was sent by Henry V to offer a pardon to their old enemy but Owain refused. In 1416 his son Meredith, now a Lancastrian courtier, accompanied Talbot on a second mission but once again Owain spurned a pardon.

Where was he? How did he die and when? The question

remains unanswered but the *Iolo Manuscript* again tells a curious tale.

At the time of Owain's disappearance there was a priest at Kentchurch in Herefordshire. The living was in the gift of Sir John Skydmore who was by this time married to Glyndŵr's daughter. Across the valley from their home at Kentchurch Court were the ruins of Grosmont where the Children had suffered their gravest defeat and not far away was the Yellow Pool where Owain's brother had been killed and his son captured. The Priest, John of Kentchurch, was a poet with — like Glyndŵr — a reputation as a wizard. On his death-bed he wrote a poem part of which reads:

> The torment of subduing vengeance
> Alas is afflicting me.
> Woe to the one, woe to the many
> Who shall endure a portion of my torture
> Hear my groaning and sorely complaining,
> Like a wolf on a chain.
> Do not heavenly Lord I beseech thee
> Take me from the world in a state of burning.
> God of heaven forgive me the sins
> I have committed so long;
> Before dying — before the fierce summons of death
> My day it is approaching.

A heavy weight of sin on a country priest? The poem recalls the dying request of Henry IV for the Miserere to be sung with its prayer for forgiveness of blood guilt. At Kentchurch Court there is a painting, dated to the 15th century, of John of Kentchurch.

In the 19th century among the members of the Scudamore family, whose descendants live there still, there was a tradition that it was a painting of Owain Glyndŵr.

APPENDIX A

The Tri-Partite Indenture

In the first place that these lords, Owyn, the Earl and Edmund shall be mutually joined, confederated, united and bound by the bond of true league and true friendship and sure and good union.

Again that every one of these lords shall will and pursue, and also procure, the honour and welfare of one and other, and shall in good faith, hinder any losses and distresses which shall come to his knowledge by anyone whatsoever intended to be inflicted on either of them. Everyone also of them shall act and do with one another all and every of those things, which ought to be done by good and faithful friends to good and faithful friends laying aside all deceit and fraud. Also that if ever any of the said lords shall know or learn of any loss or damage intended against another by any persons whatsoever, he shall signify it to the others as speedily as possible and assist them in that particular, that each may take such measures as may seem good against such malicious purposes; and that they shall be anxious to prevent such injuries in good faith; also that they shall assist each other to the utmost of their power in time of need. Also if by God's appointment it should appear to the said Lords in process of time that they are the same persons of whom the prophet speaks, between whom the Government of the Greater Britain ought to be divided and parted then they and everyone of them shall labour to their utmost to bring this effectually to be accomplished.

Each of them, also, shall be content with that portion of the kingdom aforesaid, limited as below, without further exaction of superiority; yea, each of them in such portion assigned to him shall enjoy liberty. Also between the Lords it is unanimously covenanted and agreed that the said Owyn and his heirs shall have the whole of Cambria or Wales, by the borders, limits and boundaries underwritten, divided from Loegria which is commonly called England . . . '

The divisions of the kingdom are listed (see body of book) and the indenture continues:

Indenture 2

'Also should any battle, riot or discord fall out between two of the said lords (may it never be) then the third of the said lords, calling himself good and faithful counsel, shall duly rectify such discord riot and battle, whose approval or sentence the discordant parties shall be held bound to obey. They shall also be faithful to defend the kingdom against all men; saving only the oath on the part of the said Owen given to the Most Illustrious Prince Charles, by the Grace of God, King of the French, in the league and covenant between them made.'

APPENDIX B

The Pennal Manifesto. Written to Charles VI from Pennal on March 31.

'Whereas most illustrious prince the underwritten articles especially concern our state and the reformation and usefulness of the Church in Wales, we humbly pray that you will graciously consider it worthy to advance their object even in the Court of the said Lord Benedict.

'That the Church of St David's shall be restored to its original dignity which from the time of St David, Archbishop and Confessor, was a metropolitan church. Again that the same Lord Benedict shall appoint for the metropolitan church of St David's and the other cathedral church of our Principality, prelates, dignitaries and beneficed clergy and curates who know our language.

'Again that the Lord Benedict shall revoke and annul all incorporations, unions, connections, appropriations and parochial

churches of our Principality how so far, by any authority whatsoever with English monasteries and colleges that the true patrons
of these churches shall have the power to present to the
ordinaries of these places suitable persons to the same or appoint
others.

'Again that the said Lord Benedict shall concede to us and our
heirs, the Princes of Wales, that our chapels etc shall be free and
shall rejoice in the privileges, exemptions and immunities in
which they rejoiced in the times of our forefathers, the Princes of
Wales.

'Again that we shall have two universities or places of general
study, namely one in North Wales and the other in South Wales,
in cities, towns or places to be hereafter decided and determined
by our nuncios and ambassadors for that purpose.'

Owain demanded that Henry and his adherents should be
branded as heretics 'and cause to be tortured in the usual manner
Henry of Lancaster and his adherents in that of their own free
will they had burned or caused to be burned so many cathedrals,
contents and parish churches.'

BIBLIOGRAPHY

The Chronicles

— Of Adam of Usk.

— Of Capgrave.

— Of Dieulares Abbey.

— Of Jean Creton.

— Of John Hardyng.

— Of St Albans.

— Of Hollinshead.

— Of William Stewart.

— Of Incert Auctoris.

— Of St Denys.

— Of Walsingham.

— Of Matthew of Paris.

— Of the Monk of Evesham.

— Of Sir John Froissart.

— Of Enguerrand de Monstrellet. Translated Thomas Johnes (1810)

General History.

Some 15th century history relating to Montgomery
  — Montgomeryshire Collection.

History of the English Speaking People
  — W. S. Churchill (Purnell Edition)

Wales Through the Ages Vol. I
  — Ed. A. J. Roderick

History of Chester
  — Hemingway

The Island Kingdoms
  — Bryant

Costumes and Fashion
  — Norris

English Costume
  — Pat Cooke

The Arts in the Middle Ages
  — Paul Lacroix

Henry IV
  — John Lavan Kirby

Westminster Hall
  — Hilary St G. Saunders

History of England under Henry IV
  — A. J. Wylie

Mediæval Wales
  — R. Ian Jack

Historie de la Reigne de Charles VI
  — Maselle de Lussan

François Villon
  — D. B. Wyndham Lewis

Brief Lives
— John Aubrey

Speculum Vol. XV
— E. J. Jones

Henry IV and the Percies
— J. M. W. Bean

Archaeologia
— Professor J. E. Lloyd

The Penguin Book of Welsh Verse
— Anthony Conran (Ed.)

Wild Wales
— George Borrow

It All Happened Before
— John Radnor

The Late Middle Ages
— A. R. Myers

The Fifteenth Century
— E. F. Jacob

The Fine Art of Food
— Ray Tannahill

The Public Records Office.

Ancient Indictments of the King's Bench.

Gaol Delivery Roll, Justices Itinerant.

Formal Plea Rolls of the King's Bench and Common Pleas.

Early Chancery Proceedings.

The Biographies.

Memoirs of Owen Glendower, a supplement to a History of Anglesey
— Thomas Ellis (1775)

Owen Glendower, a supplement to Tours in Wales
— Thomas Pennant (1825)

Owen Glyn Dŵr
— A. G. Bradley (1901)

Owen Glendower
— J. E. Lloyd (1931)

Owen Glyn Dŵr
— Griffiths Davies (1934)

Owain Glyndŵr
— Glanmor Williams (1966)

Supplementary Bibliographical Research.

Bulletin of the Board of Celtic Studies XX (1963)

Bulletin of the Institute of Historical Research (1964)
— Articles in both the above by Dr Ralph A. Griffiths.

The Grey of Ruthin Valour
— R. Ian Jack

Owain Glyndŵr and the Lordship of Ruthin
— R. Ian Jack

Transcript and Descriptive List of the Mediæval Court Rolls of the Marcher Lordship of Clun
— Thesis by G. E. A. Raspin

Welsh History Review
— I. J. Jones

The Court of Common Pleas in the 15th Century
— M. Hastings

Owain Glyndŵr's Raid on Ruthin
— Transactions of the Denbighshire Historical Society

Letters and Documents

Calendar of Ancient Correspondence Concerning Wales
— (Board of Celtic Studies, History and Law Series Vol. 2)
1935

Proceedings and Ordinances of the Privy Council
— Edited by Sir H. Nicholas (1834)

Anglo Norman Letters and Petitions
— M. D. Legge

Royal Letters of Henry IV (1860)

Original Letters Illustrative of English History Vol. I
— H. Ellis (1827)

Documents of British History
— Douglas

A Documentary History of England
— Bagley and Rowley

Iolo Manuscript

Military History and Tactics

The Art of War in the Middle Ages
— C. W. C. Olman

Military and Religious Life in the Middle Ages
— Lacroix

Laws of War in the Late Middle Ages
— M. H. Keen

Society at War
— C. T. Allmand

The Organisation of War Under Edward III
   — R. J. Hewitt

General Ordinances of War, the Black Book of the Admiralty,
Rolls Series

Muster and Review
   — R. A. Newhall

An Account of the Castle and Town of Ruthin
   — Canon R. Newcombe

Harlech Castle

Rhuddlan Castle   Official guide books of the

Beaumaris Castle   Department of the
                         Environment

Caernarvon Castle

The Battlefields of England

The Book of the Ordyre of Chyualry
   — Ed. A. T. P. Byles (1926)

The Book of Fayttes of Arms and of Chyualry of Christine de
Pisan
   — Ed. A. T. P. Byles (1937)

INDEX

A

Abberley Hill, 157
Aberdaron, David of, dean of Bangor, 137, 147
Abergavenny, 49, 85, 115, 159
Abergavenny, Lord, 49, 134
Aberystwyth, 76, 97, 167, 168, 169
Acton, Roger, 95
Albany, duke of, 52, 162, 163
Alleyn Thomas and John, 141
Alman, Thomas of Poppleton, 150, 151
Anglesey, 37, 42, 44, 82, 119, 124, 145
Aquinas, Thomas, 70
Archibald the Grim, see, Douglas, earl of
Arthur, king, 34, 79, 155
Arundel, earls of, 17, 18, 57, 86, 121, 140, 150, 155
Arundel, Thomas, archbishop of Canterbury, 12, 15, 78, 150
Astwick, John, 31
Augustine, St, 70
Aumarle, duke of, 16

B

Bala, 33
Baldwin, archbishop of Canterbury, 36
Banbury, Essex, 77
Bangor, 38, 123
Bardsey, abbot of, 38
Barry, Gerald de, 36, 43
Beauchamp, Richard, see Warwick, earl of
Beauchamp, William, 115
Beaufort, John, earl of Somerset, 38, 75, 96, 161
Beaumaris, 38, 42, 44, 119, 122, 145, 160
Bell, John le, 62
Benedict XIII, Pope, 165, 166
Bere, Kinard de la, 83
Berkely, Lord, 155, 167
Berkerolles, Lady, 177
Berkerolles, Sir Lawrence, 176, 177
Berwick, 45, 84, 173

Berwyn Mountains, 17, 31
Black Prince, the, 12, 43, 54, 63, 68, 174
Blount, Sir Walter, 113
Bodenham, John, 98
Bolde, John, 73
Borrow, George, 19
Boucicault, marshal of France, 18
Bower (historian), 52
Brecon, 76, 98, 99, 100, 101, 117, 125, 126, 136
Bretton, 106
Bridlington, John of, 12
Bristol, 17, 63, 119, 139, 167
Britonley, Hugh de, 34
Bromshull, William, 141
Browe, Monsieur Hugh, 57
Bryn Glâs, battle of, 83
Brynlluarth, 33
Builth Wells, 33, 75
Burgundy, duke of, 85, 127, 163
Burgundy, John, duke of (son), 163
Burnell, Hugh, Sheriff of Welshpool, 36
Burton, Sir John, 123
Byfort, Lewis, bishop of Bangor, 123, 124, 147, 165, 172

C

Cader Idris, 57, 82
Cadfan, heroes of, 34
Cadogan of the Battle Axe, 124
Caerleon, 85, 103, 121, 135, 155
Caernarvon, 42, 44, 55, 73, 81, 82, 118, 119, 122
Caerphilly, 121
Cambr, Peers, 26
Cambridge, 39, 53, 174
Canterbury, archbishop of, 53, 150; see also Arundel, Thomas
Capenhurst, Thomas de, 81, 82
Capgrave, Thomas, 83
Cardiff, 85, 121, 135, 177
Cardigan, 76, 144

Carewe, Thomas earl of, 101, 103
Carmarthen, 13, 76, 99, 101, 103, 155, 160, 161
Carreg Cennen Castle, 54, 101, 161
Carrick, James, earl of, 162, 163
Carrog, 19, 31, 33, 34, 80
Catherine, aunt of Glyndŵr, 32
Caw of Edernion, 34
Caxton, William, 71
Ceiriog Valley, 25
Charles V, king of France, 70, 130
Charles VI, king of France, 90, 127, 129, 130, 131, 162, 164-167
Charlton, John, Sieur of Powis, 58, 76
Charlton, Sir Edward, Sieur of Powis, 49, 61, 76, 82, 136, 164, 171, 172
Chaucer, Geoffrey, 14, 84, 95
Chaucer, Thomas, 50
Chester, 17, 23, 24, 27, 36, 61, 66, 74, 81, 82, 86, 95, 99, 101, 103, 107, 118, 138, 141, 164, 173, 174
Chester, earl of, 23
'Children', Owain's, 36, 60-62, 70, 72, 75, 81, 145, 177, 178
Chirk, 25, 26
Chirkland, March of, 17, 26
Christine the Pisan, 70, 71, 140, 169
Clark, Petronilla, 104
Clanvow, Thomas, 84, 95
Clarence, Lionel, duke of, 59, 137
Clarendon, Sir Roger, 54
Clares, the, 17
Clark, William (of Chester), 53
Clwyd, Vale of (Dyffryn Clwyd), 33, 34, 123, 141
Coedmarchan, 35, 79
Conway, 16, 42-48, 118, 122
Conwy, Owen, 50, 51
Corbie, Arnaud de, 132
Corwen, 17, 31, 33
Couele, John, 50
Coventry, 37
'Crab', a poet, 31, 32, 38
Crécy, battle of, 42, 153
Criccieth, 42
Croesau, 17, 38
Cwm Llannerch, 83
Cymer, abbey of, 60
Cymer, abbot of, 38, 126
Cynllaith Owain, 17, 33

D

Dee, River, 12. 17, 19, 31, 82, 87, 95, 117
Denbigh, 33, 36, 44, 82
Derby, 148
Despencer, Countess Constance, 139, 140, 141
Despencer, Lord, 139
Devereux, Walter, 83
Dinas Brân, 31
Dolgellau, 126, 129
Don, Henry, of Kidwelly, 48, 99, 100, 117, 119
Donald, Lord of the Isles, 52
Douglas, earl of (Archibald the Grim), 28, 89-93, 111, 113, 114
Douglas, Margaret, 28
Drosselan Castle, 101
Dunbar, Elizabeth, 28
Dunbar, George, earl of Scottish March, 28, 89, 90
Dynevor Castle, 99, 100

E

Edeirnion, 33, 96
Edward I, king, 21, 24, 33, 36, 42, 123
Edward III, king, 54, 59, 137, 148
Edwyn, Richard, 78
Eglwysig, 31
Evan, Griffith ap, 31

F

Faireford, John, 99, 100, 102
Fitz Pers, John, 49
Fitzalans, family of, 17
Flemings, 59, 60, 101, 103, 104
Flint Castle, 12, 36, 42, 44, 66, 122
France, 47, 84, 94, 122, 129-133, 135, 139, 153, 154, 162-164
Franciscans, 53, 77, 177
Froissart, Sir John, 63
Fulthorpe, Sir William, 150
Fychan, Evan, 31
Fychan, Llywelyn ap Gruffydd, 17, 32

G

Gam, Davy, 54, 125, 126, 177
Gascoigne, Lord Chief Justice, 149, 150
Gaunt, John of, 12, 19, 126, 154
Gethin, Rhys, 83, 99, 124, 135

Gifford, John, 33
Gilberts, family of, 17
Glyndŵr, Alice, 54, 62, 161
Glyndŵr, Catherine, 62, 84, 171
Glyndŵr, Griffith, 31, 63, 142, 143, 144, 171
Glyndŵr, Helen, 32
Glyndŵr, John, 62
Glyndŵr, Madoc, 62
Glyndŵr, Margaret, 17, 171
Glyndŵr, Meredith, 62, 171, 177
Glyndŵr, Owain, quarrel with Grey of Ruthin, 16, 17, 22-25, 24-30; his boyhood, 17-18; home life, 19-21; coronation, 31-32; attack on Ruthin, 34-36; 'Children's' raids on border castles, 36; outlawed, 38; recruits army to deliver Wales, 48-49; supporters at Oxford, 49-52; funds for, 53, 54, 122, 159-161; Hotspur's victory against, 57; escapes capture, 58; victory over Flemings, 59-60; sacks Radnor and Cymer Abbey, 60-61; landowners pledge allegiance to, 62; asks Scotland and Ireland for help, 69; leads raids in North Wales, 72; attacks Caernarvon Castle, 73; makes peace overtures to Henry IV, 74-75; captures Grey of Ruthin, 79; demands ransom for Grey, 80-81; triumphant in South Wales, 84-85; traitor reveals stronghold of, 86; power over elements, 88; alliance with Percys, 93; Prince of Wales takes field against, 94-99; his army captures Carmarthen, 101; consults Master of Brut, 103; captures Earl of March, 110; in command in Wales, 117-121; his court at Harlech, 123-125; his parliament and coronation, 125; and Davy Gam, 126; tries to raise European support, 127; sends emissaries to France, 129; treaty with France, 132-133; Bishop Trevor joins his cause, 134; ascendancy admitted by Privy Council, 136; and Tripartite Indenture, 137-138; and plot to bring Earl of March to Wales, 139; attack on Usk and defeat at Battle of Pwll Melyn, 142-146; and the Scrope Conspiracy, 147; and the French Invasion, 154-155, 158; alliance with Duke of Orleans, 163, 164; support sought for Avignon Pope, 165; his plans for reorganisation of Church in Wales and for establishment of Universities, 166; at bay in Harlech Castle, 167; anger at fall of Aberystwyth, 168; and siege of Harlech, 171; escape from Harlech, 171; reverts to guerilla tactics, 172-173; last defeat at Welshpool in 1410, 173; legends concerning, 176-177; offered pardon by Henry V, 177; disappearance of, 178
Glyndŵr, Thomas, 62
Glyndŵr, Tudor, 19, 31, 38, 142, 143
Glyndyfrdwy, 17, 19, 29, 33, 96
Gower, 103, 144
Grassington, Robert, 14
Great Whitley, 157
Gregory XIII, Pope, 165
Grey, of Condor, Lord, 143, 144
Grey, of Ruthin, Lord, 15-17, 22, 25-30, 33, 35, 36, 38, 75, 79, 80, 81
Grey, Sir Richard de, 80
Greyndor, Sir John, 93, 95, 121, 135, 143, 144, 167
Griffith, Griffith ap Dafydd ap, 25, 26, 27, 28
Griffiths, Rhys ap (ap Llewellyn), 99, 100, 101, 172
Griffiths, Sir John, 149
Grosmont, 135, 142, 167, 178
Grosvenor, Robert, 19
Gruffydd, Evan ab Einion ap, 55
Gwn, (Gwyn) Gryffyth ap, 126-127
Gyffin, Howel, dean of St Asaph, 31

H

Hallow, Edmund, earl of Kent, 139
Hals, Sir Hugh, 80
Hanard, Jenkin, 99, 101
Hanmer, Griffith, 31
Hanmer, John, 124, 129-132
Hanmer, Philip, 31, 124, 172
Hardyng (chronicler), 80, 84, 88, 105, 106
Harlech, 42, 55, 74, 81, 82, 97, 117-119, 123-125, 130, 154, 167-171
Harlescott, 107, 108
Hartleigh, Kent, 80
Haverford, 155
Hawarden, 36
Hengest, Jean of, Lord of Hugeville, 127, 153, 154
Hennore, John, 117
Henry II, king, 36
Henry IV, king, succeeds Richard II, 11, 12; his first parliament, 13-14; his coronation, 15; demands return of royal baggage, 16; at battle of Radcote Bridge,

18; and Bishop Trevor, 22; attack on Chester with rebel army, 23; and Grey of Ruthin, 25; meeting with Dunbar, 28; puts down rebellion in Wales, 37-39; and Massy, 42; correspondence with Hotspur, 45; correspondence with his son, 46; faces growing power of Glyndŵr, 48; trouble with Welsh students at Oxford, 49-51; and campaign for return of Richard II, 52-53; and the Percys, 58, 59; his depleted treasury, 61; summons army at Worcester, 62-63; and Ireland, 69; his revenge against rebels, 71; his army guided by Llywelyn, 72; destroys Strata Florida, 73; received peace offer from Glyndŵr, 74, 75; and comets, 77-78; learns of defeat at Bryn Glâs, 84; rift with Hotspur, 85; autumn campaign of 1402, 87-89; hears of Humbleton Hill victory, 93; marches to help Percys, 101; correspondence with allies, 102; Hotspur turns against him, 104, 105; at battle of Shrewsbury, 108-115; receives pleas for protection against Glyndŵr, 115-117; his relations with France, 120; transfers command of Welsh War to Prince of Wales, 121-122; receives petition from Adam of Usk, 125; association with Davy Gam, 126; enmity with France, 127; correspondence with Duke of Orleans, 129; alliance against him of Owain and France, 132-133; his power declines, 134-136; and Tripartite Alliance, 137, 138; and plot to remove Earl of March from his custody, 139, 140; his army assembles at Hereford for new offensive, 146; and the Scrope Conspiracy, 147-152; and the French invasion, 154; at Woodbury Hill, 157-158; takes action against Glyndŵr's agents, 159-161; puts Scottish heir in Tower, 163-164; fights war on four fronts, 164; plans last progress into Wales, 168; death of, 174; tomb of, 175; mystery surrounding his coffin, 176; request for Miserère at funeral, 178

Henry V, king, see also Henry, Prince of Wales, 68, 161, 177

Henry, Prince of Wales, Grey's correspondence with, 27; his own Investiture contrasted with Glyndŵr's, 32; marches into Wales with father's army, 37; with Hotspur, 44, 45; his correspondence with his father, 46, 48, 62; mystic banner made into nightshirt for, 58; rebels seize his horses and tents, 72; receives offer of submission from Glyndŵr, 74; advice from Northumberland, 82; leads army into North Wales from Chester, 85-86; takes field against Glyndŵr, 94-98; at battle of Shrewsbury, 106, 112-114; in Chester, 117; takes over command of Welsh War, 121; withdraws to Worcester, 134; atacks Welsh at Grosmont, 135; attempts to stop smuggling to Welsh, 141; attacks Rhys the Black, 167; raises siege of Aberystwyth, 168; and siege of Harlech, 171

Hereford, 17, 86, 115, 116, 117, 134, 145, 146, 154, 157, 164, 168

Hertford, 78

Hiraethog, Gwilym (poet), 143, 144

Holinshead, chronicler, 77, 83

Holland, Robin of Eglwys Fach, 117

Holt, 36

Hopkyn ap Thomas of Gower, 103

Horkesley, Richard, 112

Hotspur, Harry, 44, 45-49, 57-59, 81, 82, 84, 85, 89, 92, 93, 95, 98, 99, 101, 103-115, 122, 148, 152, 158

Howel, David ap Llewelyn ap, see Gam, Davy

Howel, Howel ap Einion ap, 34

Howell, Rev. John ap, 52

Howell, Sir, of the Battle Axe, 54, 55

Huail, son of Caw of Edernion, 34

Humbleton Hill, battle of, 90, 91, 93, 107, 112, 113, 152

Hundred Years War, 14, 25, 63, 64

Hunt, William, 117

Hyddgen Valley, 59

Hywel Dda, king, 25, 125

Hywel, John ap, abbot of Llantarnam, 142, 143, 144-145

I

Iolo Goch, 19, 29, 30, 124

Irby, John, 57

Ireland, 16, 47, 69, 70, 164

Isabelle, Queen of England, 127, 129

Isabelle, Queen of France, 127, 131, 163

Isle of Man, 58

J

Jakes, Walter, 78
John, king of France, 64, 153

K

Kent, earl of 13
Kent, earl of, see Hallow, Edmund
Kentchurch, John of, 178
Kentchurch Court, 178
Kidwelly, 99, 101, 117, 119, 161
Kinderton, the baron of, 114-115
Kingeston, Richard, 102, 111, 134
Kyffin, Howell, 49, 50, 51
Kynaston, Roger, 105
Kynaston, Thomas, 108

L

Laceys, family of 17
Lacy, John, 50
Lakin, Sir Richard, 26
Lancaster, Henry Bolingbroke, duke of, see
   Henry IV
Laugharne, 101, 103
Laurence, William, 50
Legh, Piers, 24
Leicester, 53
Lekebreth, David, 50
Lestrange, Lord, 105
Lichfield, 37, 84
Llandeilo, 100
Llandovery, 72, 76, 100
Llanfaes, 38
Llanidloes, 59
Llanllechid, rector of 38
Llansanffraid, 80
Llansillin, 19
Llechryd, Lord of, see Iolo Goch
Llewellyn, Prince, 29, 32, 33, 123
Lloyd, William, 93
Llwyd, Ellis ap Richard ap Howell ap
   Morgan, 135
London, 11, 32, 33, 38, 39, 61, 69, 75, 139,
   158, 166, 174
London, bishop of, 80
Lucy, Sir William, 49
Lugg, River, 83

M

Machynlleth, 93, 125
Madog, Madog ap Evan ab, 31
Maenan, abbot of, 38
Maidstone, William, 140
Malvern, John, 151
Marcher Lords, 25, 27, 32, 39, 48, 85
Massy, John, 42-44, 48, 114
Mawddwy, John of, 55
Maydestone, Clement, 174-175
Menai Straits, 38, 145
Meredith, Evan ap, 55
Meredith, Robert ap, 55
Merioneth, 45
Milan, duke of, 79
Milford Haven, 153, 154, 155
Molyngton, John de, 81, 82
Mona, Guy de, bishop of St David's, 75
Monmouth, 135, 142, 161
Montgomery, 61
Mortimer, Catherine, see Glyndŵr,
   Catherine
Mortimer, Edmund, 33
Mortimer, Edmund, earl of March, 59, 84,
   110, 137, 138, 139, 141
Mortimer, Sir Edmund, 74, 75, 82-85, 93,
   110, 124, 137, 167
Mortimer, Roger (brother of earl), 139,
   141
Mortimers, family of, 17, 33
Mowbray, Thomas, 148-151
Moyle family, 34

N

Neville, Thomas, Lord Furnival, 114
Newcastle-on-Tyne, 28, 173
Newport, 85, 121, 135
Norbury, John, 15
Northampton, 37
Northumberland, Henry Percy, 1st earl of,
   15, 16, 53, 74, 75, 82, 85, 105-106, 111,
   137, 138, 147-152, 171, 173
Nottingham, 103

O

Oke, John, of Newent, 158-161
Oldcastle, Sir John, 75, 95
Ordinances of War, 67, 68, 92
Orkney, earl of, 162, 163
Orleans, Louis, duke of, 85, 127, 128, 129,
   163, 164

Oswestry, 17, 26, 36, 82
Owyn, Med ap, 55
Oxford, 39, 40, 49-51, 60, 166, 175
Oxford, Robert de Vere, earl of, *see* Vere, Robert de

P

Painscastle, 76
Parliament, of October 1399, 13-15, 22; of January 1401 passes anti-Welsh legistlation, 39-40; the Merciless, 104; of Glyndŵr, 125; complains about war in Wales, 145
Parys, Robert, 118
Pay, Henry, Warden of the Cinque Ports, 155
Pennant, Thomas, 80, 138
Percy, Henry, *see* Northumberland, 1st earl of
Percy, Henry, *see* Hotspur
Percy, Sir Thomas, 16, 127
Percy, Thomas, earl of Worcester, *see* Worcester, earl of
Peris, Lake, 38, 58
Peyntour, David, 50
Philip, William ap, 99, 100
Pilleth, 83, 124
Plumpton, Sir William, 148, 149, 151
Plymouth, 119
Plynlimmon Mountain, 59
Poitiers, battle of, 54, 153
Pole Castle, 74, 172
Pole, Sir John de, 81
Powis, Meredith, 16
Powis, Sieur de, *see* Charlton, John and Sir Edward
Powis Castle, 160, 172
Powys, 31, 32
Prestbury, Thomas, abbot of Shrewsbury, 111
Puleston, Robert, 31
Pwll Melyn (the Yellow Pool), battle of, 143-146, 178

R

Radcote Bridge, battle of, 18
Radnor, 60, 121
Ramorgny, Sir John, 162
Red Iolo Llwyd, Lord of Llechryd, *see* Iolo Goch
Rede, John, 50
Renault of Trie, Admiral of France, 153

Rhôs Fawr, 38
Rhosymeirch, 145
Rhuddlan, 36, 42, 117, 122
Rhys Ddu (the Black), 98-99, 124, 167, 168, 173, 174
Rhys, the Lord, 73
Richard II, king, 11-16, 18, 22-24, 37, 42, 44, 52-55, 65, 93, 104-106, 109, 110, 121, 127, 134, 148, 151, 174
Rieux, Jean de, marshal of France, 153
Robert III, king of Scotland, 52, 69, 162-164
Robert the One Eye, 153
Rokeby, Sir Thomas, 173
Rome, 78, 81, 125, 142, 144, 149, 165, 171, 172
Roos, Sir William de, 80
Rothesay, David, duke of, 28, 161
Rufus, William, 14
Ruthin, 17, 33-35, 79, 124
Ruthin, Lord Grey of, *see* Grey, Lord

S

St Albans, 77
St Asaph, 81
St George, Master James of, 42
Saladin, 36
Salghall, John, Constable of Harlech, 55
Salvayn, Roger, 108
Savage, Arnald, 46
Savoy, Count Philip of, 42
Sawtree, Sir William, 53
Scarisbrooke, Henry, 118, 119
Scarle, John, 15
Scotland, 47, 52, 53, 55, 58, 69, 84, 89, 149, 151, 165
Scots, 19, 28, 43, 85, 89-92, 101, 164
Scottish wars, 19, 37, 66
Scrope, Lord, 19
Scrope, Richard, archbishop of York, 147, 149-151, 174
Scrope Conspiracy, 147-149, 152
Sele, Hywel, of Nannau, 54, 126, 127
Severn, River, 37, 99, 138, 156
Shrewsbury, 13, 17, 29, 37, 38, 70, 73, 84, 86, 99, 103, 106, 108, 110, 114, 115, 138, 174
Shrewsbury, battle of, 43, 104, 112-113, 118, 122, 137, 165
Six Ashes, 138
Skydmore, Alice, *see* Glyndŵr, Alice
Skydmore, Philpot, 54, 159, 172, 174
Skydmore, Sir John, 54, 101, 159, 160, 161, 178

Snowdonia, 38, 48, 59, 145
Stafford, 36, 105
Stafford, earl of, 86, 111-113
Stanley, Sir John, 154
Stanley, Sir William, 81, 117
Stewart (Scottish rhymer), 89
Stirling Castle, 52
Strangeways, James, 58
Strata Florida, abbey of, 73, 168
Sycharth, 19, 21, 31, 60, 96

T

Talbot, John, 167, 171, 173
Talbot, Lord, 29
Talbot, Sir Gilbert, 177
Taylor, Emmota, 50, 51
Taylor, Hugo, 50
Taylor, Wilfred, 50, 51
Tempest, Sir Nicholas, 173
Tenby, 155
Tiptoft, Sir Paganus, 159-160
Tirel, Guillaume, 130, 131
Trevor, John, bishop of St Asaph, 22-24, 26, 81, 133, 134, 147, 165, 173
Tripartite Indenture, 137-139
Tudors, family of, 32, 43, 124, 144, 172
Tudor, Goronwy ap, 37, 82
Tudor, Gwilym ap, 37, 42-47
Tudor, Rhys ap, 37, 42, 43, 46, 174

U

Usk, 49, 85, 87, 117, 121, 135, 142, 144
Usk, Adam of, 12, 13, 23, 24, 32, 33, 40, 47, 49, 72, 78, 79, 81, 104, 125, 142, 144, 171, 172, 176
Usk, Edward, 78

V

Vaughan, Howel, 46
Vaughan, Howell, 93
Vaughan, Robert of Hengwrt, 60
Vegetius, 71
Venables, William, deputy warden of the Marches, 118, 119
Vere, Robert de, earl of Oxford, 19
Vernon, Sir Richard, 114-115
Veyse, John, 159-161
Vychan, Griffith, 17, 32
Vyrnwy, River, 36

W

Wale, John, 26, 27
Walsingham, Thomas of, 83, 108
Walton, Walter, 14
Warwick, 36
Warwick, Richard Beauchamp, earl of, 76, 86, 167
Waterton, John, 140
Welshpool, 36, 61, 174
Westminster, Palace of, 13, 14, 32, 104, 174
Westmoreland, earl of, 15, 148, 149
Whitiford, William, 86, 89
Whitney, Robert, 83
Wilford, William of, 119, 120
Wilicotes, William, 50
Willoughby, Sir William de, 80
Winchester, Statute of, 65
Woodbury Hill, 156-158
Worcester, 62-64, 66-68, 70, 73, 134, 138, 155-158, 164, 165
Worcester, Thomas Percy, earl of, 75, 105, 109, 111, 112, 114, 115
Wye, River, 87
Wygmor, constable of Carmarthen, 99

Y

Yale, 33, 141
Yellow Pool, see Pwll Melyn
Yevèle, Henry, 14
York, 147-151, 173
York, Edmund, duke of, 121, 140, 167
York, Richard of, 134
Young, Gruffydd, 122-124, 129-132, 165, 172
Ystrad-fflur, see Strata Florida

Z

Zouche, Sir William de, 80

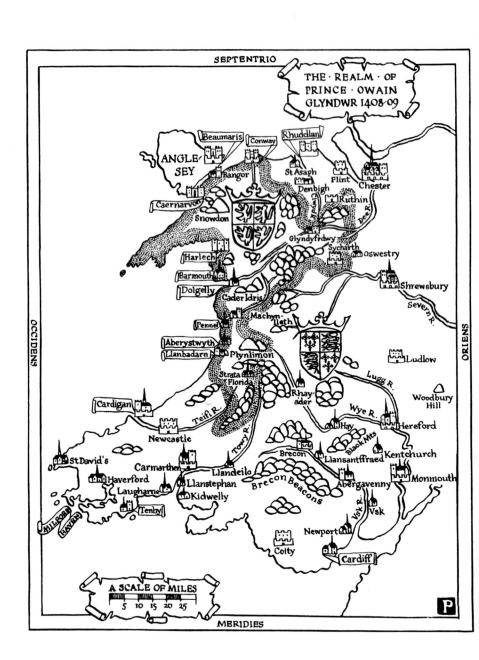

THE · REALM · OF
PRINCE · OWAIN
GLYNDWR 1408·09

SEPTENTRIO

OCCIDENS

ORIENS

MERIDIES

ANGLE·SEY

Beaumaris
Conway
Rhuddlan
Bangor
St Asaph
Flint
Chester
Caernarvon
Denbigh
Ruthin
Snowdon
Dee R.
Glyndyfrdwy
Sycharth
Oswestry
Harlech
Barmouth
Shrewsbury
Dolgelly
Severn R.
Cader Idris
Machynlleth
Pennel
Ludlow
Aberystwyth
Lugg R.
Llanbadarn
Plynlimon
Strata Florida
Rhayader
Woodbury Hill
Cardigan
Teifi R.
Wye R.
Newcastle
Towy R.
Hay
Hereford
St David's
Black Mts.
Kentchurch
Carmarthen
Brecon
Llansantffraed
Haverford
Llandeilo
Monmouth
Laugharne
Llanstephan
Brecon Beacons
Abergavenny
Kidwelly
Tenby
Usk R.
Usk
MILFORD HAVEN
Newport
Colty
Cardiff

A SCALE OF MILES
5   10 15 20 25

P

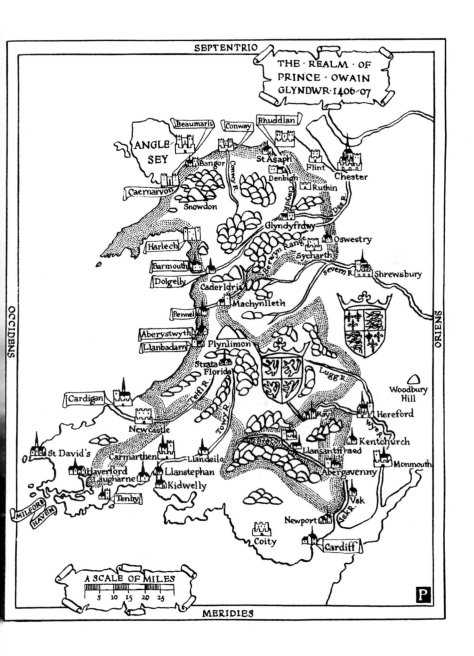

THE · REALM · OF
PRINCE · OWAIN
GLYNDWR · 1406-07

SEPTENTRIO

OCCIDENS

ORIENS

MERIDIES

ANGLESEY

Beaumaris
Conway
Rhuddlan
Bangor
St Asaph
Flint
Chester
Denbigh
Caernarvon
Ruthin
Snowdon
Conway R.
Clwyd R.
Dee R.
Glyndyfrdwy
Oswestry
Berwyn Range
Sycharth
Harlech
Barmouth
Severn R.
Shrewsbury
Dolgelly
Cader Idris
Machynlleth
Pennel
Aberystwyth
Llanbadarn
Plynlimon
Strata Florida
Lugg R.
Teifi R.
Woodbury Hill
Cardigan
Towy R.
Hay
Hereford
Newcastle
Kentchurch
Wye R.
St David's
Carmarthen
Llandeilo
Llansantffraed
Monmouth
Haverford
Laugharne
Llanstephan
Abergavenny
Kidwelly
Tenby
Usk
MILFORD HAVEN
Newport
Usk R.
Coity
Cardiff

A SCALE OF MILES
5 10 15 20 25

P